# Schooled

*A Teacher's Memoir*

Reba Saxon

Village Scribes Publishing
AUSTIN, TEXAS

Copyright © 2014 by Reba Saxon.

All rights reserved. No part of this publication may be reproduced, distributed or transmitted in any form or by any means, including photocopying, recording, or other electronic or mechanical methods, without the prior written permission of the publisher, except in the case of brief quotations embodied in critical reviews and certain other noncommercial uses permitted by copyright law. For permission requests, write to the publisher, addressed "Attention: Permissions Coordinator," at the address below.

Village Scribes Publishing
PO Box 170343
Austin, Texas 78717
www.villagescribes.com

Book Layout ©2014 BookDesignTemplates.com

Ordering Information:
Quantity sales. Special discounts are available on quantity purchases by corporations, associations, and others. For details, contact sales@villagescribes.com

Library of Congress Cataloging-in-Publication Data

Saxon, Reba

Schooled / by Reba Saxon: Teaching memoir. C. 2010.

ISBN: 978-0-9831436-9-7 (trade paperback; alk. paper)

1. Teaching—United States. I. Saxon, Reba. Schooled: A Teacher's Memoir. II. Title. III. A Teaching Memoir.

# Prologue

This book may sound like sour grapes, but I don't want it to. I want you to think here was a creative, dynamic teacher—not just someone who was a credit to her profession, but someone who could make real changes. And she is no longer in the school system. And I want you to think that's a shame.

I hope this book will start you thinking about some things. If you are an administrator maybe you know this, but you should start advocating for teachers instead of everyone but teachers. People will stay if they believe they are valued.

If you are a student, knowing what is going on in the teacher's head should help you to make better use of everyone's time in class, and paying attention to how you learn will give you the words you need to tell a teacher that you need a different way to learn something, if that's the case. Seek out the best teachers; only your parents will have more impact on your life, and you can't choose them.

If you are a parent, step up to the plate and parent your children, dammit! Don't wait for the schools to teach them right from wrong, what it means to be a good person or citizen. Do everything you can to vote, canvass for school bonds, lobby the legislature, talk on social media about the fact that we must pay teachers better so they can stay in the schools and gain experience and wisdom to pass back to your children. They must be able to afford to raise their own families, or they have to leave. Simple as that.

And if you are considering the teaching profession, or in school already to enter it, think long and hard about the time you are spending and make sure that it will pay off. Make sure that the place where you teach and the people in it are good for you

Four years for a college degree, maybe six for a Master's. Four years of teaching. Leave teaching. Five years later, still paying student loans. That was me, and that's the experience of nearly half of those who enter the teaching profession today. Biggest contributing factors: lack of control over your own work and unmanageable workloads. We are burying teachers under the responsibilities that our society doesn't want, and the burden of documenting that they are doing it.

My mission is not to keep potential teachers out of education, but to encourage engagement in a real dialogue about what is wrong with schools in general and with teaching as a profession. Our society has foisted off many of its responsibilities onto the school system, our legal system has mandated and dehumanized it, and teachers are the ones who bear the burden. They are typically people who enjoy helping others, who can't say no and so are being taken advantage of by a society no longer able to address what to do with its members when they are not capable or willing participants. If you are thinking of entering the teaching profession, I want you to come in with your eyes open and know what you are getting into. Teaching is—at its core—a very worthwhile career, and can make you float with happiness and excitement when what you do really makes a difference for a person. There are not many jobs that can do that. But along with that ability to float, you will receive sandbags tied to you: administrators, parents, and unwilling students.

    Bon voyage!

Reba Saxon

# Part One
Student

## { 1 }

# Elementary: The Making of a Teacher

I saw the classroom in a dream the night before I got there. My father died of a heart attack at 36, leaving my mother with me at six years old, and my 2-year old brother, far, far from her family in a neighboring state. So she moved us—not quite to the tiny town where most of her family was, but to the nearby larger city to seek whatever advantages she could find there and hopefully get some help and support from her family. It ended up being secretarial school and a little free family babysitting, bless her heart.

Daddy died on December 21, so following a very strange Christmas when I received gifts from a father who was no longer there, we moved during Christmas break and relocated me to my new school to start at the beginning of the new year. My first memory of school is entering that classroom after dreaming it the night before, complete with the girl with dark braids, freckles, and wide blue eyes sitting at the desk paired beside mine. I was only mildly surprised to see her there, as the previous couple of weeks had been a turmoil of chaos, sorrow, a complete inability to understand, and a deep desire to just go on up and see my Daddy in Heaven where all of the adults told me we would be reunited. A bit surreal. So when I saw that girl, I just thought, "Oh, so this can happen, too."

That night I reported on my first day at the dinner table where my mother and Granny sat with my little brother. Granny was staying with us for a little while, helping Mom get settled from the move and its tragic reason. I regaled them with the day's events, including the hysterical joke I saw written on the bathroom stall door. It must have been a joke and mighty funny, I just didn't know what it meant and was too busy being grown up and able to handle everything to let them know that. So I told them, "You won't believe the joke I saw on the bathroom door: it said 'Fuck Mrs. Anthony!'" I added a hearty laugh. My mother's jaw hit the table. She couldn't speak—I don't think she could inhale. Granny said to her, "She doesn't know what she's saying, she doesn't know what she's saying!" I guess after thirteen kids, Granny knew a thing or two.

First grade was tiresome. Reading is a lot of what is required and expected. It takes up a lot of time. No matter how teachers teach it—phonics, reading aloud, through writing, puzzles, or activities—kids either know how to read when they start first grade, 'get it' at some point in the fall, or come back from Christmas break knowing how to read. One teacher told me, "It's a rain dance. We just do a lot of dancing and take credit for the rain when it comes."

I had learned to read before kindergarten, by memorizing books like *Muggsy the Dog* and *The Three Bears*. Well, I could fake reading by reciting the words to Daddy and turning the pages at the right time. But over time, I memorized the words and taught myself. Kindergarten just polished it up so I knew how to read when I came to first grade. I just wanted to learn how to do *real* writing, meaning cursive. I knew that was how adults wrote, and I already had the printing thing down. I kept complaining to the teacher, asking just when she would get around to teaching us *real writing*, and she handed me more busywork.

Our house faced a hill and when cars rounded the curve in front of our house at the bottom, the only protection was three huge mimosa trees. Mimosas are very easy to climb, with large low limbs, and their feathery leaf fronds cast a dappled shade that is most comfortable in the Southern heat, particularly before we had air conditioning. We did have an attic fan that would draw the hot air in from all the open windows, making you think that a warm breeze was better than nothing. Within the next year or two, we got a window air conditioner, and Mother put it in the den with a recliner in front of it. That was the throne, no question about it.

I started a private school in those mimosa trees. My students, younger children from the neighborhood, took their seats solemnly on their respective branches and I provided them with pads of paper and pencils or crayons. I boasted that yes, I did know how to do real writing, and would proceed to teach them how to write their own names in real writing. I had them watch as I carefully wound the pencil around in a loopy imitation of what cursive writing would look like if letters were not required. I then assigned them the copying of the example, at least seven times. My 3-5 year-old students performed these copies meticulously, tongue-tips waving up and down out of the sides of their mouths. For these valuable lessons, I charged them a quarter. I should have kept it to a nickel, because the moms in the neighborhood started questioning my students on how they had spent their entire week's allowance so quickly, without even going down to the Pak-a-Sak.

Mother heard about it from an irate neighbor and made me quit the private school business, so I had to turn to sales to make my living as a 6-year old, picking dewberries in the wild parts of woods and vacant lots, and selling them door-to-door. If they wouldn't buy, I cried right there on the doorstep. That worked. I was always a great closer. If the mimosa school was my start in teaching, the dewberry business was my start in sales.

Second grade was just more first grade work, still no real writing, so I simply left one day and walked home because I was done with it until I could go to third grade when, I had just been told, I would actually be taught real writing. The school noticed I was missing, called my mom, and she arrived at home in such a panic that I stoically agreed to continue with second grade even if they were only rehashing first. I still have little patience with poorly-paced instruction, and have formed many of my opinions about education from that two-year lull waiting for what I wanted to learn, what was *relevant to me*.

I did finally learn how to "do real writing" in third grade but the rest of elementary was a blur educationally. Except for New Math. New Math was a new way of counting on your fingers in 0s and 1s, binary they called it, and it made everything very difficult because you had to translate before you solved the problem, then translate back out of New Math to give the answer. But guess what runs on 0s and 1s? Computers. So I guess someone was learning it, like those government guys and IBM, followed by Bill Gates and Steve Jobs.

I do remember Chinese jump-rope, which was done through and around a long band of elastic held in a narrow rectangle by the ankles of two holders about six feet apart. I was a champion jump-roper, anyway, and Chinese jump-rope was even more fun, with the group of holders and waiting jumpers clapping rhythms and chanting for the jumper. I was also hell on the tetherball court. These days, I look at elementary schoolyards and they have large, puffy-looking playground equipment made of hard colorful plastic. We had slightly rusty metal monkey bars, swings with really long chains so we could fly off at the top of the arc and really get some height before we crashed to the hard ground, and a good long metal slide, unusable when it was hot without pants, which girls were not allowed to wear.

I remember the news of JFK's assassination being told to us in fourth grade, how we all looked around the room at each other, blinking, some kids started crying. I don't know if they sent us home from school or if they just told us right at the end and then it was time to go home, but I remember the feeling of shock walking home, like you were wrapped up in cotton and couldn't quite connect to anything like before, like the world had suddenly changed. And it had.

And I remember the Duck and Cover drills meant to teach us how to protect ourselves in the event of a nearby nuclear bomb blast. We were certain it would be us. Every community was. Every community had something those damn Russkies would want to destroy. We had Barksdale Air Force Base, though, so we knew there was a bulls-eye painted on our town on the map. Our teachers said so. In the event of a bright flash, you were to hide under your school desk, not run to the window to be shredded by flying glass as it broke from the percussive blast. They never explained that last part, though, so I assumed that the desk would be protecting me from the radioactive fallout from the mushroom cloud I had seen on TV. I was so unnerved by these drills that I slowly stocked the car with pilfered cans of food from our pantry, thinking that if a bomb were to go off we just might have time to jump in the car, roll up the windows, and drive very fast to a safe place out of range of the radioactivity. In other words outrun a nuclear blast. One day Mom slammed on the brakes and all the cans of green beans and creamed corn rolled out under her feet. I had to remove them, so my only chance at that point was if the bomb hit while I was in school so I would have the protection of my desk.

{ 2 }

# Junior High: The Making of an Idealist

"You look dead," Rich Becky told me. I was standing on the top step of the portable classroom, in line to get my school yearbook picture taken. One of the few times I would be standing this close to a popular girl, and only by virtue of the alphabet. I was not very good with makeup, in fact didn't own any yet when I saw an ad in Seventeen Magazine for a Bonne Bell Makeup Sampler package in a round striped tube for just $1. It arrived in the mail and contained tiny tubes of foundation, white concealer, mascara, a tiny super-frosted lipstick and "10-0-6 Lotion", Bonne Bell's claim to fame, a strong astringent applied with cotton pads that removed miraculous amounts of oil and dirt even after you had washed with soap. Twelve-year-old girls are suddenly beset with oily skin, breasts, and a period, in rapid order. I hardly knew what could happen next.

All makeup was pale then, I thought. It was all about London's Carnaby Street, with the thinnest of all models, Twiggy, in her almost white eye shadow and lipstick being held up as the ideal. I used the white concealer as eye shadow, not knowing any better, and the super pale lipstick. I thought I looked great. Rich Becky, tall, slim, well-groomed, probably didn't like the fact that we shared the same first name and considered me a blot on Beckyhood. Girls can be stunningly cruel.

It's funny how places you spent time in your youth stay with you as dreamscapes for the rest of your life. My junior high is one for me. My memories mostly revolve around gym class because I hated it. The locker room, where I had to disrobe before strangers for the first time in my life, the mannish gym teacher who drove us to excel at the President's fitness test, volleyball, softball and tumbling. I was best at the fitness test, as I am way too short to spike the volleyball and a doofus when it comes to catching anything, to the extent that I somehow allowed a softball to hit me in the head so hard I was knocked out. I warned her I shouldn't be playing softball. Probably the most vivid memory is being pushed into a laundry cart while I was trying to change out of my gymsuit and then shoved into the boys' shop class across the outdoor hall in my underwear. Squeek, squeeeek, squee-ee-ee-ek went the wheels of the cart as it slowly came to a stop in the middle of the table saws, drillpresses and speechless wide-eyed boys. I had to clamber up and over the edge of the cart and run out, in flames of embarrassment that lasted—well, really I'm still embarrassed when I remember it.

But the physical plant of the place is so clear: every locker-lined hallway, a couple of the classrooms, the breezeways outside the cafeteria and the gym, the circle where Mom or a carpool mom picked me up every day. When I visit my hometown and drive by, a sense of familiarity comes over me just looking at it from the front, like I could walk inside and everything would be the same. I have had so many dreams of myself at all stages of life that take place in that hallway, between those two buildings, or at that entrance to the portable, where I was standing when Becky let me know I would never, never be a regular woman.

Adolescent idealism is a recognized stage of life, but sometimes events hurl themselves at us earlier to bring us to that sensibility. As we mature, when our world starts to encompass the one beyond our family and friends, we get an understanding of abstract concepts like Justice, and become morally outraged when we learn about wrongs happening. This is what comic books and superheroes prepare us for at an earlier age. While I was busy becoming a nonconformist, becoming an 'intellectual', becoming a pacifist and becoming a woman, daily events made it seem as though chaos was the best we could hope for. War, civil rights, political assassinations, serial killers, Beatles, Doors, Rolling Stones, drugs, Summer of Love all leading up to the big shebang, 1968.

Here's a brief overview of the events that might have shaped the newly formed morals and ideals of a 14-year old that year alone, in order: the Vietnam War really went sour with the Tet Offensive and the Mai Lai Massacre, LBJ announced he wouldn't run for re-election, *2001: A Space Odyssey* opened on April 2, then on April 4 Martin Luther King was assassinated. Student protestors shut down Columbia University by taking over the administration buildings, civil rights marchers were shot by American policemen, race riots in major cities, the musical Hair opened on Broadway, Robert Kennedy was killed only a month after MLK, the Chicago 7 protests at the Democratic National Convention, Yale decided to admit women, in November after LBJ announced he would be withdrawing troops from Vietnam we went ahead and dropped three million tons of bombs on the Ho Chi Minh Trail, a PanAm flight was hijacked to Cuba, and Apollo 8 capped off the year with a look at the far side of the moon. You didn't know whether you were coming or going with all these things happening one right after the other.

Some people shut down, refusing to move forward in such a crazy world. Drugs like marijuana and LSD were readily available, so escape was easy and peer-sanctioned. Some people became politicized, with the urgent desire to get out of their small town where no one understood them and participate in the 'Revolution'.

I straddled both camps, but at 14 I wasn't going anywhere yet. So I internalized all these conflicts, trying to make sense of them. My friends' older brothers were in danger of being drafted to fight in a war we did not believe in. Many of them went to college in those years just to avoid the draft.

Looking back, it's easy to see why I ended up a liberal. I was once told that if you are not a liberal when you are young you have no heart, and if you are not a conservative when you are older you have no brain. I guess I have no brain, because I am still moved by my heart more than my brain in moral issues. Most of the jobs I've had in my life have ended on moral grounds. It's always the principle of the thing.

Mom married an alcoholic and they fought whenever he was drunk, which was most of the time. Screaming arguments in her bedroom rang through the house. My younger brother cowering in his bed could hear everything through the wall his room shared with hers. The temporary husband would storm out, grabbing his daiquiri blender and slamming the door, to go stay in the tiny apartment in his warehouse across the state line in Texas. Then Mom would get a glass of sauterne, retire to the formal living room and close the sliding doors, crying and listening to Nat King Cole. Once my mother, brother and I sat down to a quiet spaghetti dinner when the temp roared in, drunk as Cooter Brown. He swayed in a small circle in the kitchen as we stared across the breakfast bar with forks suspended in midair, then he passed out on the floor. We all three burst out laughing.

Sneaking out was popular. Boys would come and knock on my bedroom window. After furtive whispered encouragement through a two-inch opening in the window, my best friend Cathy and I would creep through the living room and out the front door. We walked around the neighborhood in the dark, once or twice "papered" someone's house with toilet paper thrown over the big pine trees. There wasn't a whole lot to do since no one could drive yet, so we would sneak back in after a couple of hours and Mom was never the wiser. Until one night when the temp stormed out with his naked pot belly hanging over his boxer shorts. "I've got a gun! I'm calling the police!"

I would have done anything at that point to get him to go back inside, so running was not an option since he'd probably try to follow. Once inside, he bellowed at me, "You'd better mind me, young lady! I'm your father!" Which of course let me establish in no uncertain terms that no, he was not my father, never would be my father, and was embarrassing. The marriage didn't last long after that, and Mom just went back to widowhood, boyfriends and weekend dates.

For extra spending money, I babysat the small children across the street, including an infant so I learned diapering. This convinced me that I really didn't want children when I grew up. There was a little boy next door whom I really loved, though. He was very intelligent, and I think no one else really talked to him like a person instead of a 5-year old. He would come over to my house, knock on the door, and ask my mother if I could play, meaning come outside and sit on the front lawn and talk. He had a complete theology made up from what he understood in church.

"See those clouds up there?"

"Uh-huh."

"Those clouds are in Heaven."

"What's Heaven?"

He looked at me like I had lost my mind. "God and Jesus *live* in Heaven."

"Oh, really?"

"Yep. Jesus is Mrs. God. She drives a Mustang."

He had it all figured out. I think my respect for kids' ideas probably started with him. And I might like to go to Heaven if I, too, could drive a Mustang there.

{ 3 }

# High School: Big Society

We walked through empty halls of a closed high school, eerie echoes of our footsteps bouncing off new walls, chalkboards, desks and chairs. We were on a field trip to visit the closed school whose black students were bused to ours. Busing was a big issue we had heard about in the news and our parents' conversations. My speech teacher had arranged this trip so that we could see what those other kids on the buses had to give up. I was already not a bigot, preferring to distance myself as much as possible from the redneck norm. Realizing that the black kids had to leave their perfectly good high school in their own neighborhood, ride a bus five miles (too far to walk or ride a bike) to the white high school, and put up with a bunch of sullen white kids intent on making them miserable put me in a different frame of mind. A mind out for Justice. For 17 years after Brown vs Board of Education, Louisiana had firmly insisted that providing equal educational opportunities was okay, but it could still be in different *places*. In 1971, the Supreme Court ruled unanimously that forced busing of students would be used to achieve desegregation, overruling state laws of most of the South. We were in the thick of it.

We had moved to the southeast side of town when I was in sixth grade, where the white areas were much larger, not the patchwork of black and white areas that had evolved naturally on the west side. New neighborhoods were springing up in former cotton fields and my mother purchased a new to-be-built home in Broadmoor Terrace. The first house on the street, way at the outer edge, still surrounded by fields the first year until others were built on our block. She made all of the decisions on floor plan, brick and paint colors herself. Not bad for a widowed single mom in 1965. She had started a new job, as secretary for a successful real estate broker, and in a couple of years would become a real estate agent herself.

Five years later I was a junior in high school and one of the 'freaks'—hippie wannabes who didn't fit in as academics or athletes, but weren't nerds either. We were the music, art, book and theatre crowd. Okay, nerds, but art nerds. After feeling like an outcast in junior high I found myself in the theatre and became a theatre rat, there all the time.

High school theatre productions are serious six-week affairs with rehearsals every night, real sets on a real stage in a real theatre, not the "cafetorium" of elementary and junior high. I had a role in every production, learned how to use tools by building sets, how to sew by making costumes.

We theatre rats somehow got ourselves into a Creative Writing class, too. That was my first writing experience, and the teacher was wise enough to just let us go, see what we could do, and then point out what we had done well. Probably informed my teaching the poetry class many years later. We were all A students, so we wrangled off-campus passes for research and spent most mornings getting jittery on black coffee in the only coffee shop in the area. It was us and a bunch of blue-uniformed postmen. We felt like beatniks.

Our high school was new the year before, an odd circular building that looked very architecturally avant-garde for its time, rising up out of the cotton fields. The shape caused a lot of running to class, because if you missed your classroom and you were already running you just kept going around the circle until you came to it again. It was faster than turning around against the momentum.

The school was built to service all the new white neighborhoods, so the eastside white children wouldn't have to attend C.E. Byrd, the school that was already "mixed" in the center of town. About the same time, a new school was built in the middle of the black neighborhoods. This was the prescient city fathers' hedge against having their children attend with black kids, since they could complain about the distance to the homes being a justification for keeping things the way they were.

The Supreme Court decision in 1971 threw Louisiana into a spotlight, and busing was mandated mid-year. Rumors flew that we white kids might be the busees and have to attend the black school, but of course that didn't happen. The black school was closed and the students were just moved to a kind of school-within-a-school in ours. We shared no academic classes at first, just P.E. The schools claimed they were "tracking", grouping students by ability so they could be taught better. The very valid idea of tracking is used in many countries to create different curricula for students who want to go on to a college track and others who want to move into a trade. But the segregationist misuse of the concept back in the '70s gave tracking a black eye from which it has never recovered in the US.

White parents warned us not to drink from the water fountains, since there were no separate ones for the "niggers" (and yes, they used that word). The black kids themselves were bewildered, frightened, wary and sometimes belligerent to mask it. A week passed before they organized themselves, but then over the weekend they must have talked and formed a plan. The next Monday they refused to get off the buses. Police were called, and the commotion stopped classes inside. I ran down to join them, along with a couple of other white kids. We were doing what we saw in the civil rights marches that Walter Cronkite showed us. "Hell, no! We won't go!"

We only lasted a few minutes before the principal quickly nabbed us by the shoulders and demanded that we go to his office. It took about an hour before he and the police had everything sorted out, the black kids' buses sent back to their homes for the day to return the next. When he called me in to sit across from his desk, it was my first time ever in the principal's office.

"Becky, I'm disappointed in you. You are a good student! I may have to expel you for this!"

I caved quickly. I had successfully avoided capture smoking cigarettes in the bathroom, but that was my only misdemeanor at school. Expulsion would be a blot on my family for years to come ("We may have to move!"), not like today when it's practically a rite of passage. He suspended me for the rest of the day, and I somehow kept Mom from ever finding out. I guess they had bigger fish to fry than getting in touch with one of the few moms who didn't answer their phone because they were at work.

After a while, the new situation started to feel normal again. Over a few years, the black kids were assimilated into the classes. Some turned out to be valedictorian-smart, and the athletes gained acceptance for their whole race by making our formerly all-white football and basketball teams into champions. If not for their prowess, whites might still be fighting segregation today. I became good friends with one boy who was a like a black panther on the basketball court. He moved with a sure grace that was different from any of the other players, black or white. He was the star, but he was quiet and reserved.

We met in the parking lot one day, skipping class. If you didn't have a car to get off campus for your skipping, all you could do was just avoid class and stay there. One of the best places to pass the time was in a car in the parking lot, any car since no one locked their doors then. If things had been different, I would have allowed myself to be in love with Jeff, but we settled for great conversations.

One of the most interesting things about Jeff was that he *hated* basketball. It was just a tall black kid's ticket to college, so he had started practicing when he was little for that reason only. Now he was big, very big, well over six feet tall. We became good friends in the halls as well as skipping classes, and it became known in the black crowd that I was okay because I was Jeff's friend. It saved me from a locker room fight when I bumped the elbow of a girl built like Serena Williams who had a locker next to mine. She had a temper like Serena's, too, and was known to be a fighter. She spun me back and started yelling, "Do you have a problem with me? Huh?" when another girl grabbed her and whispered something in her ear, most likely that I was Jeff's friend. She instantly backed off, smoldering, but no longer threatening. I had no more problems with black kids.

# { 4 }

# High School: Small Society

I did get into a fight in high school. Best friend Cathy was over to spend the night, and Mom dropped us off to cruise the shopping center. It was a giant L-shaped strip center. (This was pre-mall.) The Woolworth's five-and-dime was a favorite hangout because it had a diner counter in the corner and you could get an order of French fries and a Coke for less than a dollar. Since it was right across from Stan's Record Shop where you could buy a Number-1 hit 45rpm record for 65 cents, this was well within range of a teenager on $2.50 allowance.

In the Woolworth's checkout line, we bumped into three other girls from school. Laurie lived down the street from me, and I knew her well. Sandy was a cheerleader and I was surprised to see them together, but much more surprised to see them with Ginger Watson, a hefty mean girl who was known as a fighter. She had snatched my friend Billie by her red hair in the stairwell and dragged her down it. Cathy and I had just giggled over the false eyelash display that looked like a bunch of black furry caterpillars in plastic packages. When I looked up and saw the other three girls, Ginger was wearing a similar pair and must have thought I was making a joke about her.

When Cathy and I arrived back at my house later that afternoon, Laurie called to see if we wanted to come over. We strolled down the block and walked through the open front door, then through the den where Laurie's older brother Stephen was watching TV in the recliner. His look at us was strange, I noted, like he wanted to say something but couldn't. We went upstairs to Laurie's room where she and Sandy were on the two twin beds. Everyone brought out cigarettes and as soon as they were lit, the tiny half-height door from Laurie's room into the attic space opened slowly and Ginger sat there cross-legged like a Buddha.

She unfolded herself, walked into the bedroom, and sat down beside me, snatching my lit cigarette from me and starting to smoke it. On cue, Laurie and Sandy grabbed Cathy's arms and led her down the hall toward the stairs. I thought, "Okay, I'll wait here.

It's fine if she takes that cigarette, I'll just light another one for myself." When I looked up from the package, a fist flew at my face and hit me square between the eyes.

"Wait! I'm a girl!" I thought, "This can't be happening to me!" But it was and she was cranking up for another one. I had no idea how to hit back, but saw Ginger's long hair swing around her side as she was winding up for the punch. I grabbed the hair and she howled, obviously very tender-headed. I pulled the hank of hair down and held her bent to the side. She yelled, "Let go!"

"Not 'til you let me out of this room!" and I walked, connected to Ginger by that hank of hair held down below our waists, dragging her with me all the way out the bedroom door, down the long hall and to the top of the stairs until I let go and ran down and out of the house, Cathy right behind me. We ran all the way to my house, into my bedroom, and slammed the door.

Mom found us trying to put a steak on my eye, like we had seen in cartoons. I had to tell her what had happened. She insisted on calling the police. "We'll put a peace bond out on her so that if she gets near you they'll arrest her!"

"No! That will only make it worse! She'll beat me up before they get there. Just leave it alone, Mom!"

As it turned out, that was the best choice. I never even saw Ginger except from a distance for the rest of that year, and you can believe I gave her a wide berth when I did. The next year, when I was a senior, my usual smoking lounge restroom was closed for repairs and I went to another one I had never used. Ginger was there. She was showing some photos she had taken to another girl and obviously didn't recognize me.

I had taken a photography course in a city program, and enjoyed composition and the darkroom. I asked her if I could have a look. Her portfolio contained idyllic pictures of a little girl in a field of daisies, almost saccharine-sweet. I said, "These are nice," and Ginger looked me in the eyes, recognizing me. Everything stopped, nothing was said. We went back to looking at the photos.

The last thing I ever heard about Ginger was later that year when her father blew his brains out in the front yard with a shotgun. A friend who lived in her neighborhood, a low-income rural pocket of town, told me that it was well known that he was a monster, beating his wife and kids all the time. The neighbors had heard it all. He had been a drill sergeant at Barksdale AFB. That explained it: fighting and violence was just another way of communicating, sometimes the only attention Ginger could get. She was, after all, that little girl in the daisies.

## { 5 }

# College: New Orleans

"**M**aybe you should get a degree in teaching or something, in case this theatre thing doesn't work out," my mother told me. Well, that put the kibosh on teaching, because I WAS going to be an actor! That would be admitting defeat before I even tried! I went to college in New Orleans, at what is now called the University of New Orleans. Back then it was Louisiana State University at New Orleans, but they got tired of getting shorted on funding and seeing it all go to the LSU football and basketball programs, so they broke off and dropped the Louisiana State part. I almost flunked the first year, 18 years old and living in New Orleans, for heaven's sake. I'm not saying I didn't learn anything; I learned how to drink legally in bars. Back home in Shreveport, the legal drinking age of eighteen hadn't stopped our local package liquor stores from operating their profitable businesses however they saw fit. Some even had drive-up service for mixed drinks, where you had a speaker to order and a waitress brought out the drinks. I am sure that this service was used to circumvent some requirement that if the drink orderer was standing in front of you, you had to ask them how old they were. If the order was coming in over a speaker, how could you?

The second year in New Orleans wasn't much better academically. I declared a theatre major, moved out of the dorms and shared an apartment with a gay friend from Shreveport. Gay men make the best roommates. They care about the apartment, can cook and clean at least as well as any girl I know, but aren't trying to get you in the sack all the time. I began to learn how to cook differently from my mom's Depression-Baby Rural Southern style in which everything is fried—including bread, vegetables, meats, and desserts. I copied recipes from New Orleans restaurants, friends and their families, and watched Julia Child as a delightful break from Watergate hearings.

My first apartment of my own was Uptown, in a black working-class neighborhood. Some people might say that wouldn't be a good place for a 20-year old white girl, but I never felt safer. My apartment was in a two-story house on one side of the second story. The only other apartment was the other side. The first floor was just storage, like a basement but actual basements don't exist in New Orleans because the water table is nine feet above the city. Massive municipal pumping stations pump the water out of the city so it can exist. You remember Katrina. The flooding was as awful as it was because the pumping stations were out. And you've probably heard about the "charming" old cemeteries of mausoleums there, how everyone is buried that way because caskets would float up out of the ground. Anyway, the living area was on the second floor, with a huge Southern porch across the front and a grand staircase with curved sides up to the porch from the sidewalk. The apartment was up in the trees on the second floor, and the jungle greenness of New Orleans burst through every window.

My neighbor was the only other white person in the neighborhood. Armand was a big good-looking hippie poet, with blond curly hair to his shoulders. He reminded me of Robert Plant, the Led Zeppelin singer. He had been in the neighborhood for a while and had become known as someone who would go with the locals to a government office and get better attention for them if they needed it. He went to the Social Security office with the little old men who hung out on their stoops and drank wine all day. Imagine a big hippie with his palms on your desk, standing over you and yelling, "I don't CARE if 'he's just going to drink it.' It's HIS MONEY!" Very effective. So the apartment was a charmed space when I got there, lovingly protected by Armand's constituency.

I became the neighborhood teacher. (Something about me and kids up in trees.) They came to sprawl out on my front or back porches on their bellies, coloring in coloring books with 128-Crayola boxes. The big box. With the sharpener. They didn't come inside, just came to visit outside. It started with the ones next door, then they told their friends. I read to them sometimes, helped with their penmanship homework on Big Chief tablets. If I was busy cleaning or cooking, they loved to just color in a fresh coloring book, one with so many choices of pages. No selections ruined with scribbles by a younger brother or sister.

We talked, of course, about the world and the things they thought about and about the relative merits of outlining with a darker line of crayon vs just trying to stay inside the lines by stopping short of the black ones. Which one was more realistic? In short, we respected each other.

Four of them came to my screen door one day, breathlessly trying to outdo each other in luring me to help a cat they had seen up in a tree. They insisted I had to come right away and help that cat.

"That cat can get down on his own. I'm busy."

"No, ma'am! He's way up there, he cain't get down! You have to come help!"

I wondered if they thought I would climb a tree myself to save this ragged feline.

"Have you ever seen a kitty's skeleton up in a tree?"

"Noooo."

"Well, then, I assure you that if you leave that cat alone he will jump down and be just fine."

"Can we use your phone to call the fire department?"

Oh, so that was it. Excitement in the neighborhood.

When the fire engine wailed into the next block, I smiled, happy they hadn't given my address.

# { 6 }

# School Tools

I have always loved the tools of school. Every year in August when we went shopping for school supplies was like Christmas shopping for me. I got excited, even as an adult, allowing myself a new package of pens while shopping for all the items on my sons' supply list provided by their teachers. I even enjoyed the jostling of the carts in the one aisle devoted to every item on all the lists, not just notebooks, backpacks, pens, pencils, but also boxes of tissue, baggies, and other items that the teacher knows she will need and doesn't have in her budget. I love comparison shopping for pens: gel? ball-point? Sharpie? with sponge finger grips? black or blue? And pencils: good old wood? need a sharpener? mechanical? what lead size? Even glue: is the store brand as good as Elmer's? Has anyone come up with a cap design that will keep glue sticks from drying out in a month? Whatever happened to LePage's Paste, with the really salty taste? (Yes, I was a paste-eater.) Staplers, 3-hole punches, compasses, rulers, notebook paper (is he ready for college-ruled, and its greater demand for content?) And TABS! I love tabs! They make you feel so organized! I told my high school students that if they would just use tabs I wouldn't even read their paper, I would just give them an A because it showed organization. Nobody ever took me up on it.

Things have vastly changed since I was in grade school. For one thing, I loved the smell of mimeographs so much that I held them up to my face and inhaled them when they were passed out just after printing. You know that was toxic. Now, we have computers (laptop, netbook, desktop, Mac, PC?) and printers, so cheap to produce they are given away with computer purchases, hoping to hook you into using their ink cartridges which cost as much as a whole new printer, rendering the printers disposable but not recyclable, like razors and razorblades.

I think one of the reasons I like writing so much is that it keeps me in the school supply aisle, but some of the physical tools of teaching I am glad to be rid of. Those heinous deskal-chair things that never really fit anyone. I'm convinced they were invented by a teacher who was bound and determined to stop students from leaning back in their chairs. Cartridge pens guaranteed to leak, and the first BIC stick pens that always accumulated a blob of ink on the tip, just waiting to blot an otherwise perfect paper or finger just prior to the finger's scratching something on your face. I am pretty happy about the absence of chalkboards, too. I could never stand the bone-buzzing feeling of writing with chalk, and I mean any writing with chalk, not just when you hold it at the wrong angle and it screeches. I'm not sure that dry erase markers are an improvement, as they can run out of ink at the very most wrong moment and permanent markers seem to jump into your hand and maliciously stain the board when you meant to use the erasable one. I do love postit notes but I'm not sure they are an improvement, since for someone with Attention Deficit Disorder like me they just provide unfileable documents with fragmentary information that is not really really reliably attached to its place on a document. They are like Twitter tweets of the paper world, though, and indispensable to a writer because of their forced brevity.

Reba Saxon

# Part Two
## Student Becomes Teacher

{ 7 }

# Choosing Teaching

Everything is sales, and I mean everything. Education, politics, parenting, religion, medicine. Much of human interaction is persuasion—persuading someone to think or do something you want them to think or do. I had been in sales, marketing and publishing for fifteen years when I decided to stay home with my babies until they went to school. When it was time to go back to work, I felt like I wanted to do something *more* with my life than sales. I had a higher calling. I decided that I either wanted to be a teacher or a nurse. It was later, after looking up in the classroom one day and realizing that what I was doing was selling, that I came to know the basic fact that I am a really good salesperson and should just use that.

The nurse idea came to me because I loved the births of my two sons. The first was born so quickly that by the time I was really scared that it was going to get worse than it already was I was whisked into the delivery room, too late for drugs. That was it, the zenith of the pain, it did not get any worse. It stayed at that crescendo level for the duration but the birth was quick, a couple of pushes and then the high that comes afterward when you are so relieved and in love you are ready to have another one right away.

I arranged to give birth to my second son at home with the professional assistance of a very good friend who was a midwife. I wouldn't trade that experience for anything. It was so much better to go through labor at home, when you can't decide if you need to pee/throw up/walk around/crawl/shit all at the same time or at least in very quick succession, but you are in your own home and on your own bathroom floor, thank you God. Being right there at home when the birth was done, laying there in the glow after the burst of joy when they are out and they are alright, in your own bed, looking up at your own ceiling, with your darling new love object laying there beside you. I loved the whole process. After that great experience I was considering becoming a Labor & Delivery nurse, so I went up to the hospital in the middle of the night and interviewed all of the nurses I could find, on all the floors.

They were universally unhappy, except for ICU (Intensive Care Unit) and Labor & Delivery. All of the other nurses had been removed a layer from actual bedside nursing. They were running groups of lesser-educated nurses' aides, being sent to classes to learn litigation-proof report-writing and were now managers, which they had not entered the nursing profession to be. But ICU and Labor & Delivery were still working directly with their patients, and were all happy in their jobs.

I've thought a lot about that particular pairing, and use it as a metaphor for working in real estate now. Being an ICU nurse is like working with sellers, because they act as though you are attempting to draw dollars out of their bodies like blood when you suggest that the price at which they want to list their home is too high, or that perhaps they will have to remove additional flotsam or actually work on their landscape. The buyers, though, are Labor & Delivery: they are happy, excited, nervous, and when you are there at closing they are happy, happy, happy: we're getting a new baby!

I tried nursing by entering college to pick up the courses I would need. I knew I had to really beef up the science, since I had none in my liberal arts transcript. I started out with a basic biology course at a community college, which happened to have a famous professor from Denmark who wanted to teach in a small rural community college so he could have a chance to live in New Mexico for a while. The first class was my last.

"You won't be seeing me again but I just wanted to let you know it's not you, it's me," I told him at the end of that class, like we were breaking up. It was just that the material assumed that the students were maybe a year or two from their last high school biology class and remembered some of it, and I was over twenty years out and did not. That, coupled with the realization that I really *am* a liberal arts person and just not that good at science, ended my nursing career.

Teaching turned out to be a much better fit. I finished a very lengthy college career at my seventh college, University of New Mexico, with a Secondary Language Arts Education degree, which qualified me to teach just about anything that wasn't math or science. I loved it. I did have to come up with some science or math to flesh out my graduation plan. I had an advisor who figured out that I could do one of the two, math or science, and qualify for the degree. I think they changed that the year after I locked it in so that you had to do both. Good thing, too, because although I can do simple math without a calculator I never could grasp the graphing that went with upper levels of math.

I only had one college math credit from way back when I had started in college, and it was Math for Liberal Arts Majors. We didn't really *do* any math, we just talked about guys who did. Copernicus, Galileo, it was like a biography class on mathematicians. It counted for college credit, but I was sure I couldn't go on to take two more math classes, so science it was. I chose geology and loved it—everything in New Mexico is thrust up out of the ground for you, the mountains, valleys, craters, riverbeds, all there to create delight, thrilling you with your ability to identify them and providing new awe at the wonders of how this planet got to look this way by studying how those mountains got there.

I felt mentally alive again in a way I hadn't since I had been in a classroom as a student. That's the key if you are what is called "learning-based", you just love the educative process no matter where you are in it. As a student, as a teacher, doesn't matter. Just being a part of an interactive community involved in a common goal of learning about a particular topic is at least ten times as much fun as watching television by yourself.

I was an excellent student, studying the two years to complete my teaching degree, top of the class and highly recommended by professors, while driving an hour and a half each way to the classes. I took all my classes on Tuesdays and Thursdays, and it worked out fine except for one dicey drive home in a snowstorm. This all started when I got my second son into preschool those two days a week, at age four.

I loved the classes, the collegial atmosphere of the students and teachers, everything about it. I graduated with a 4.0, pulling my total GPA from six other schools over twenty-one years up to a 3.6. I was very proud. During the coursework, I had the opportunity to work with students for three weeks as an intern, and for a full semester as a student teacher.

{ 8 }

# Teacher Education:

# High School Intern

We lived in rural New Mexico, in a little town called Pojoaque (Po-*wa*-kay). It is in the northwest corner of Santa Fe County, and the population was 45% Hispanic, 50% Pueblo Indian, and about 5% Anglo. Since the schools were near my home, it was easy to establish a relationship with the school administration so that I could complete my practice there instead of traveling to Albuquerque to be in the schools where all of my fellow UNM classmates were student teaching. I visited two classrooms just to get a feel for it before I turned in my initial paper on what I expected to do and find.

The first visit was to the class I would be interning. We interned for six weeks before the full semester of student teaching. The school was single-story, built of red brick during the WPA administration and hadn't changed much since then, including the plumbing. At least a couple times a year the school was closed because of plumbing issues and the students and teachers were simply sent home. The teacher, a small Hispanic woman, was the head of the English department. Her students were working on reading a novel, some were turning in homework and some weren't, there was a general feeling of malaise, of just getting through something. The next visit, though, was to an honors class that was being taught using the Socratic Method, in which the teacher creates a framework on a subject or topic and the students take over and learn through designing questions which they then answer in full, rich, sophisticated ways that made me, watching, feel as though I was in a warm bath it was so wonderful. If swooning were still available as a modern response, I would have swooned.

After this exciting glimpse of how things could be once I was an experienced teacher, I checked back in with the regular class where I taught one 90-minute class during the three weeks, assisted the lead teacher, and wrote a paper on an aspect of learning.

I was captivated by the concept of multiple intelligences in my college study, the idea that we are all smart in something, some way of learning, just maybe not the way things have always been taught in school. School is really designed for people like me: people who learn by seeing or hearing something. I can gain understanding by just listening to a lecture. Write the outline on the board or power point and I get even more. But some folks don't really learn well with either of those methods; they need to do something physically, experience it in some way. That's why teachers today are very careful to incorporate activities into every curriculum, and are evaluated on how well/often they do.

Howard Gardner created the research at Harvard to prove his theory of multiple intelligences, and although some of it has been refuted since, I still think it provides a good explanation for why people learn differently. Gardner initially identified eight different ways that people learn. These include the linguistic and logical/mathematical ways that school traditionally uses, but also kinesthetic, musical, social (interpersonal and intrapersonal), and environmental. You can't really teach everything using all eight all the time, but you can remember to use the Big Three: listening, seeing, and doing, and I think with humans you must also incorporate the social method as well, which I interpret as using stories.

Gardner completed his research with adults since they are easier to come by than children when it comes to research in a university setting. Identifying which is your dominant intelligence or 'way of learning' was done through an aptitude test, in which you answer questions about what activities you like to do and rank how much you like them. The tests that I found for this were definitely written for adults, with questions including options for playing bridge or golf among other old-fogey activities. I searched for a test I could use on teenagers and couldn't find one so I wrote one to fit their activities, adapting the ones for adults with activities like going to the mall and playing cards instead of golf and bridge. Today I'm sure that video games would provide a major area of interest.

The focus on multiple intelligences came to me during one of those initial visits to the middle school. The class was reading *Farewell to Manzanar,* a short novel about the Japanese internment camps in California during WWII. The students were called on to take turns reading aloud and of course some were much better at this than others. Since my son is dyslexic, this always makes me cringe to watch.

I was sitting in the back of the room, and the girl in the back row in front of me seemed completely detached, maybe to avoid being called on to read out loud. She was restless, switching from laying her head down on one arm on the desk to flopping her long black hair over and laying her head on the other arm, alternating between drifting off to sleep and swinging her leg. I was convinced she was not even listening.

Reading time over, the teacher instructed the students to come up, get a piece of butcher paper off the big roll, and draw the camp as it was described in the book. The girl came to life, almost ran to the front to get paper, and immediately started her sketch back at her desk. She had everything right, every building, fence and gate, very detailed, and was obviously happy to be able to prove what she knew. Now, what if that teacher had only allowed the students to get credit through a pop quiz or other written test? The girl would certainly not have been as excited to comply, and I wondered if she could even express how she knew so much by answering someone else's questions.

Multiple intelligences was the perfect subject for my one class to teach in the internship. Back at the high school, I taught a class on the concept, the students completed the assessment, scored it, and were able to determine their primary way of learning. Then they wrote a response to that new knowledge: Did they think it was correct or incorrect? Did it explain anything about them? How did they think they could apply this new information to their future learning? For example, if one knows that he/she learns best kinesthetically, it is a great benefit to be able to tell a teacher who is only offering the information visually that you need to learn it in a different, more hands-on way. It was a huge success. The kids loved to learn something about themselves, they all felt they could use the new information in future school efforts, and they enthusiastically wrote great essay pieces about their experience.

# { 9 }

# Student Teaching:

# Middle School

The high school and middle school principals got together and decided that middle school was where they needed the free assistance of a student teacher the most. The main thing I learned teaching middle school was that I would tear my hair out before I would teach middle school for a living. I was definitely a high school teacher. The saying in the biz is that if you teach kids you teach elementary or middle school, and if you teach your discipline you teach high school or college. They're that different.

    I was asked by my lead teacher to take on the job of teaching a bunch of eighth-grade hellions grammar. This would take the onerous subject off her plate and allow her to do things that were much more fun, stimulating, and teachable. She was no dummy. Far from it, in fact. Melissa was a young, beautiful ball of fire. She had real ideas about how to engage students on a much higher plane than what normally happens in a poorly-funded rural classroom. Topped with a big head of long curly brown hair, with electric blue eyes, she never sat down. She looked like a tiny elfin queen, dancing around the classroom.

The teaching of grammar to the general population is a waste of time. No one but an English major will ever care what a gerund is. By the way, it is a verb used as a noun, as in "Napping is a good thing." Now you'll never forget that, will you? Such an elegant, easy explanation. But diagramming sentences? Knowing the difference between transigent and intransigent verbs? Not necessary for a full, educated life even including reading and writing. Grammar became popular in the 1800s when English teachers felt they couldn't compete with the objectivity of science and math. There were no right answers in the way that 4 is the absolute and only answer for "What is 2+2?" In English, there was always that squishy factor in grading the subjective response of the teacher to the way a student handled the subject of an essay or even the teacher's response to the subject itself. Introducing the study of grammar provided English teachers a way to get the chip off their shoulder, to be as important and calculable as math or science. There *were* absolute right answers that could be scored, thank heavens!

Today, parents want grammar taught to their children and some complain if it is not a part of the curriculum. By gosh, if I had to do it, little Vanessa will, too! What they really want, though, is an increasing level of sophistication in their student's writing and speech. They want that mightily. Every time their son or daughter uses "to be like" instead of "said, felt, thought, screamed, cowered, laughed," or any of a hundred other verbs. "I was like...and then he was like...and I'm like...and he's like..." It is very difficult to change the speech patterns of a teenager. Think back.

But with writing, there it is on the page, it can be diagrammed to show the dependent and independent clauses, the adverbs and adjectives can be counted and this is what they want: evidence that school is working. You don't have to mash people's minds into grammar to teach them that. You can just teach them sentence-combining, a method used to hook together more ideas in sentences by using transitions, punctuation, and clauses. That's it. That's all they need. Their writing can be objectively judged (graded) based on transitions, punctuation, and sentence length; it looks and sounds much better and more adult. That's what parents want, and thus what schools want, or should want. Thankfully, it seemed to make everyone happy.

I found this out while trying to teach those eighth-graders grammar in Melissa's class. She was worn out with trying to maintain order while teaching thirty bags of raging hormones grammar, the most boring thing that English could come up with. So when the word went out that there was an opportunity to have a student teacher in the English department, she jumped at it.

Melissa had many great ideas about teaching other parts of the subject: understanding fiction, writing, communication skills. She just felt that she had to teach a certain amount of grammar and hated it herself. So if she could get a student teacher to take that part, she could concentrate on the other more rewarding areas. The teaching of grammar when viewed as a subject in itself is dull, and dull is the last thing you want to have as your stool and whip with a class of eighth graders. The boys become insolent, have too much energy to burn and start picking at each other and the teacher, and the girls just zone out. I realize that I am generalizing here, and yes, some girls get jerky and some boys zone out, but the preponderance is the other way around so that's how I'll describe it.

When Melissa brightly told me that I would get to teach them grammar, I started in on diagramming and the vocabulary of words about grammar. I bored myself as badly as the kids. They were not looking forward to my day each week, and neither was I. After a lot of searching, I found the sentence-combining theory and it worked. Worked for parents, worked for students, worked for me.

At that point, I could focus on contributing to what Melissa was doing, and we had a blast. We worked on writing poetry, which elicited groans at first, but when we took them on a field trip to a coffeehouse in Santa Fe they got it.

This was pre-Starbucks, so the coffeehouse was literally a house. An old house with rooms lined with books and filled with comfy old chairs and couches, and coffee sold from the former kitchen. We felt like a bunch of real poets. We settled in for a writing afternoon and taught them the basic technique of the free-write, in which you just write whatever is in your head. The one requirement is that you don't stop the pen. At all. If you have to write "I don't know what to write, I don't know what to write, I don't know what to write" for ten minutes, so be it. Sooner or later your mind gets tired of that and comes up with something. After ten minutes, read over what you've written and underline anything good. Pick the best part you underlined and write on that for ten minutes. Pick the best part of that and write for ten minutes. Pick the best part of that and write for ten minutes. At this point, everyone had hand cramps. But we did a reading and the writing was powerful! The kids were stunned with what came out of their pens, and many were sold that day on the idea that they just might like writing after all.

Another of my favorite ideas of Melissa's was a communications activity. It had to do with communicating with their elders. Now, some of these kids were a bit rough, with rough parents, some of whom had gang involvement (I mean the parents). Often, the parents didn't really seem to care about the school or what their child did there, they were just happy to send them away somewhere for a good part of the day. We taught the kids a little bit of manners, like holding the door open for your mom, not sitting down until the parent was seated, and a rudimentary dance step that didn't involve grinding your bottom into your partner. Just a basic 4-step box. They groused a good bit about having to do it, but we forced them to actually touch each other in a respectful and dignified way. Then we organized a party at the school one evening. The students brought their parents and pot-luck desserts, and they did readings from their day at the coffeehouse. We had a bit of dancing, and the kids could dance with each other or ask their parent to dance. The parents were just knocked out to see their normally non-communicative sons or daughters having fun, proud of their own accomplishment, and acting like the adults they were becoming, ready or not, but also like the kids they still were, shy about their poetry and a bit gawky about the dancing. It was impossible not to be charmed, and the kids without exception were excited and charmed with themselves. Melissa won a District Teacher of the Year award for that party, well-deserved, and it became a regular part of the curriculum called Family Pride Night. Out-of-the-box thinking on how to engage kids, and how far to push them out of their own sometimes very small boxes, is what makes education come alive.

 I participated in the parent-teacher conferences for the students in our class. In middle school, although each child has more than the one teacher he/she had in elementary, the four teachers of the core subjects work together as a team. They have the same set of students and communicate about them within that team, so students don't just get lost and no one knows it.

 Once, we had a parent-teacher conference about a student who was particularly difficult to deal with. The father said, "Well, I have given up. I wash my hands of him." This kid was thirteen, and we needed help from the home side to manage him. I sat quietly, since I was only the student teacher, but I wanted to reach across the table and place my hands around the dad's neck screaming, "You can't just 'give up'! You signed up for this for 18 years!" It amazed me that he thought 'giving up' was even an option.

The real teachers tried to make him understand this, that when he said things like that he was creating the unmanageable boy in the boy's mind, but the father was dead-set on having completed his job and only waiting for the boy to be old enough to go away. So sad.

I finished my student teaching with Melissa and graduated from college with my BA degree in "Secondary Education, Communication Arts," which covers everything you can teach about stories: English, Speech, Theatre, Journalism, Creative Writing and more I would find out when I got there.

## { 10 }

# Hired

When it came time to get a job, I had to travel to do it. Through the grapevine and my own student teaching, we had discovered that the schools in New Mexico were not good, especially for small Anglo boys who were frequent targets of whichever brown group was most pissed off at the other at the time. With three out of the four members of our family involved in school, we thought we should try to move to a place with better schools. Also, we wanted to be closer to our families with our young children.

My husband's parents were expatriate retirees living in San Miguel de Allende, Mexico, a three-day drive from Santa Fe. Three days there and three days back with young children, pre-DVD, would kill you. Certainly take a big chunk out of any vacation time you were taking off.

My mother lives in northwest Louisiana, so being within a day's drive of her would put us in the Dallas/Houston/Austin range and would also cut a day off of the Mexico trip to two days each way. More manageable, or at least easier to think about. We decided that Austin was about the only place we could consider living in Texas, a big college town, not quite as conservative as all of our friends warned about Texas.

I started applying to districts in the Austin area, and reapplied when I saw openings for any of the subjects I could teach. When I applied for my Texas license, I found that with my degree in Communications Education, I could be licensed to teach Speech, Communications, Theatre, English, and Journalism. When I was applying, I knew that Theatre and Journalism required many hours outside the class schedule, with rehearsals and performances or publishing school newspapers and yearbooks. With small children still, I didn't think I was ready to teach one of those.

I could not get a call back. My resume was excellent, my letters of recommendation from everyone who had taught me or overseen my work were gushing. I began to realize that from New Mexico, this was going to be difficult. I had joined a listserv of English teachers during college, so I thought what the hell and put a message on the listserv that I was looking for a job in the Austin area, did anyone know anyone in that area who might be able to help me get an interview?

Lo and behold, someone did. I got one lead, a government teacher, whom I called and he knew someone in administration who thought they were looking for a speech teacher and passed my name on to the principal so I had at least one interview, at a high school on the north side of Austin. I set up plane and hotel reservations, kept cold-calling and got two more interviews. One with a middle school (Oh, no!) in a town about an hour away, and one with a high school on the south side of the Austin school district.

I flew to Austin and checked in to the hotel. It was an old funky place down in central Austin, which turned out to have a bit too much funk. Bathrooms unacceptable and signs of roaches. So I checked back out and found another hotel, still oldish and near the center of town.

The first interview with the referred high school principal was brief, he was a bit worried about my lack of experience, but won over by my recommendations. The job would be primarily Speech Communications, a newly-mandatory class for all students, with maybe some fill-in English classes. He said he would be interviewing a couple of other applicants. I liked him, though. He was a kindly older coach, with a wide, welcoming face.

After the first interview went well, I called my husband to come down and help me find a house. He could come at the end of the week, and I had the other two interviews scheduled for when he would be in Austin, so I had a week to explore. Instead of doing that, I had an allergy attack that made me look like Yoda, with swollen eyes to the point that one would not even open. I ended up spending most of the week in the hotel bed, with ice packs on my eyes, trying to get presentable.

When my husband arrived, we went out to the middle school in the small town and he drove around to explore the area while I was interviewing. The administrators were very interested in me, so they had to take me all around the school district to see the facilities.

The students were all white. That was what really stood out to me, having come from such a multicultural population in New Mexico. I was a bit worried about it. Although class hostility can create a less than desirable environment, I really like the dynamics of a good blend of cultures, and am not interested in white people enough to spend all of my time with them, much less in a middle school. You know how I felt about that. Middle school students are so goony and out of control that they can start something in a class that they think might be funny, and when it turns out to be either not funny or not appropriate for the teacher, they can't stop themselves so just keep going. You spend 75% of your time trying to get them to focus. That number is not an exaggeration, it may even be low.

The third interview was...interesting. The principal was a small man with a Napoleon complex. At least he had a huge control issue. There were two other teachers at the interview. One was an English teacher, the head of the department, and the other was the Journalism teacher who was leaving. That's what they were hiring for, a Journalism spot. They explained that one of the things they were looking for was someone who could prepare the yearbook for publishing. The principal had been reading about stress interviews, where you put the interviewee under stress and see how they react, so he kept asking me questions like "What makes you think you can do a yearbook if you've never done one before?"

Well, he could see from my resume that I had been in publishing for fifteen years for a newspaper publisher, a book publisher, and a magazine publisher. The secret he knew is that the yearbook printers desperately want your business, and their rep will walk you through it step by step if they need to, to get the contract for printing it. I didn't know that, of course, and the Journalism teacher looked at me as though she really wanted to end this ridiculous interview and just tell me the secret but she had been given her orders by Admiral Principal on what her role was in the interview. We interviewed for about a half hour, then took a tour of the school. It was a very nice building, a bit strange in that all of the hallways were outdoors. I guess it saves on electricity, but seemed like it would be forcing people out into very hot and very cold climates and back into classrooms unnecessarily. The journalism department had darkrooms, layout rooms, and a nice classroom. I was deciding that I did want to take it on.

We returned to the office for more stress interviewing. Abruptly, after a particularly personal question, the principal looked at me and said, "Your upper lip is getting thin. Are you upset? Are you stressed by these questions?" Hell, I felt like I was about to cry. I really didn't want to cry in the interview, so I said, "You know, if this is going to take a while, I need to go out and tell my husband that I'll need more time." It had been an hour and a half at that point.

"Oh, your husband is here? Invite him in, please, we'd like to meet him!" said Napoleon.

Warily, I went outside where Andy was waiting in the rental car. He had cruised the nearby neighborhoods for an hour and returned to pick me up. We didn't have cell phones back in those days. Some people did, but we didn't yet. I told Andy that they wanted to meet him, and he came inside.

After introductions, Andy sat down and the principal now focused on him. He shoved the yearbook toward Andy and asked him, "Do you think that your wife could do something...like this?"

I was mortified. I had no idea he would shift his unwanted attention to Andy. Andy looked at the yearbook and laughed as though he considered it a stupid question. "I don't see why not, she's done more than that." Go, Andy.

Shortly afterward, the principal offered me the job. I replied that I was grateful for the offer, but that I had a couple more interviews and needed to think about it. He said that if I didn't give him an answer right then, he couldn't guarantee the job would still be available, like a car salesman. I replied that I would have to take that chance, and we left.

In the car, I burst out crying from the release of the stress generated in the interview. Andy said, "You're not seriously considering working for someone who makes you cry, are you?" That was true, so that was it.

That afternoon, I called the first principal and told him that I wanted to take the job if it was still available. It was, so I was on my way.

{ 11 }

# First Year Teacher

The school where I first taught was only a year old. It was in a district that already had a very large high school, a district that had been designed by some powers-that-were who decided it should include both Pflugerville, the small town north of Austin that at one time had been miles away but now was side-by-side as both had grown, and the school district now included a section of Austin that abutted the town but was separated by Interstate 35. I-35 is a very significant dividing line. It runs from Canada to Mexico and is the primary north-south route through the US so it has tremendous traffic, especially 18-wheel trucks, all the time. In Austin proper it separates the rich side from the poor side, but not out by Pflugerville; it runs opposite because the entire original town was to the east. The Pflugerville School District, formerly full of fairly well-off ranchers and farmers, was not happy that they had to finance a school for part of Austin, especially a part that included numerous apartment dwellers, cityfolk, up close to and—the nerve!—even across the highway.

High school in Texas is four grade levels, 9-12. Texas uses the middle school system, with middle school containing grades 6-8 and elementary up to grade 5. This is not my favorite system. When I went to school, we had junior high instead of middle school. Elementary included 6th grade, junior high was grades 7-9, and high school grades 10,11,12. The other distinction is that in junior high, the disciplines are completely separate as in high school. The concept of middle school was formed to achieve a better transition from elementary to high school by using teams of teachers, each teaching their own discipline, but working together with one group of students and in theory through projects that are interdisciplinary, that is, they are all focused on teaching their subject using the same overarching topic, like Australia or time or weather. It has been a very successful concept; there are ten middle schools to every one junior high in the US.

I do agree with the interdisciplinary part, but the change in the grouping of grade levels doesn't take into account the range of maturity levels in reality, in my teaching practice, and in the teaching of every teacher I know.

First, 6th graders have no business in middle school. They are too young to be dealing with the requirements of four different teachers, and they certainly don't belong on school buses with 7th and 8th graders. There is a distinct shift in societal mores from ages 12 to 13, and your darling little 12-year-olds hear all of the profanity and preoccupation with sex and bathroom activities that 13 and 14 year olds specialize in. Teenagers are different from children, even at the beginning of teenhood. Sixth graders should have that year to be top dog at their elementary schools and still be nurtured a bit.

Secondly, ninth graders have no business in high school. They are just as goony as middle schoolers. They can't settle down, don't understand the difference that high school counts on a transcript. They have high school teachers who are more like professors than elementary teachers, who entered the profession to teach their discipline more than because they just love kids, and who have little patience with freshman shenanigans.

High school teachers who have been around for a while seldom teach freshmen, so 9th grade is usually shoved onto the new teachers. What this does is cause new high school teachers to question their career choice, as I did many times during my first year when the English department chair, who taught junior level honors classes (the best grade—they know how to 'do' school by then and they have more on the line than seniors who are already accepted at a college), shoved a freshman class into my Speech Communications schedule, which already contained a class with no curriculum called Multimedia. Note to self: Don't EVER teach more than two subjects at a time; teachers call these 'preps', because its not so much about the time spent in the class but the extraordinary amount of time you spend preparing for each subject with lesson plans, assessments, and constant updating to meet any new or changed requirements.

Since the school was new, we only had 9th through 11th grades. The Pflugerville School District felt that the change was too abrupt and unfair for kids who had counted all their lives on graduating from the hallowed halls of Pflugerville High, so they let the juniors who were there stay for their senior year and in the first year, they brought over the 9th and 10th graders only, who were now in the 10th and 11th grades. So we had no seniors yet; we would be growing our own, as it were.

The first day of school, I was so excited but completely unsure how to act. We had been there for a week before the students came, preparing lesson plans, putting posters up in classrooms, getting copies made for the first week. I had met the other teachers on my hall, been to a meeting on how to use the grading software. I was ready.

What I wasn't ready for was lunch. On the first day of school with actual students, lunchtime came and I went to the cafeteria. Got a tray and a salad, sat down at a table. I began to notice the other people in the cafeteria avoiding my table, swinging wide around it and looking at me oddly. I was never so happy to see anyone than two girls from my colleague's speech team, whom I had met during the prep week since they were there early helping her. They plopped down at my table and said, "You know, Mrs. Saxon, teachers don't really sit in here WITH the students."

Well, that was all I needed. I never darkened that door again, but found the Teachers Lounge where three or four male teachers could be found during any lunch period, unpacking their voluminous lunchboxes and sitting around the large table sharing sports minutiae. The women all ate Lean Cuisines or Weight Watchers Smart Ones in their rooms, coming into the lounge only for the freezer and microwave.

My classroom was on a hallway with the other speech teacher, and I was hired to supplement her numbers but that only filled out three to four periods each semester, so I was also assigned another class or two. The first semester, I got the dreaded English I.

English I means ninth graders, who are just large eighth graders. Something happens between ninth and tenth grades, for one thing our society honors this change to maturity by bestowing a driver's license. It's like the Christmas break in 1st grade, when everyone comes back able to read. Something happens at that point in the school year that we are not really responsible for, a maturing during that breather of the vacation.

Something happens the summer between ninth and tenth grade, too, that changes them from kids to young adults. Very young adults, at that point, but not nearly so goofy, understanding that school counts, and more interested in taking part in an adult way, making satirical comments, griping about the work but still doing it, finding areas of their school life that they really enjoy. Up to then, school would be fine with ninth-graders if teachers weren't there; just a chance to chat with friends all day.

In the first semester of ninth grade, they can barely be controlled. They want to chat in class, they don't want to do the work, and they want to crack wise way beyond the teacher's sense of humor and patience. They are not mature enough to know when they have overstepped bounds. I believe I quit four times during that semester. They would exasperate me so that I would announce,

"That's it! I quit!" and storm out the door, slamming it behind me. I was happy to imagine the look of shock on their faces.

Every time I did this, there was an assistant principal who happened to be in the hallway, and who really didn't want a teacher quitting in the middle of a semester. "That's alright, Mrs. Saxon, I'll step in for a while." And they would go into the classroom and scold them until I had a breather and walked back in.

Once, the juniors and seniors on my colleague's debate team, who resided next door where I often went to grouse about my class, asked me if they could have a word with the freshmen.

They really reamed them. "If you make that woman quit, we'll get you! We'll make you so miserable in this school you'll never forget it! You don't know when you've got it good! Mrs. Saxon is an excellent teacher, she works with us and she is so cool and really respects us. If you don't know how rare that is, you're idiots!" That did seem to help for a while.

Although I hated teaching this class, and actually went to the principal's office and dropped to my knees and begged not to ever have to teach it again (one of the few times I made him smile) I did meet several students in there who took classes from me all four years they were in high school. When it came time to turn in their choices for classes the following year, they would come to me and ask what I was teaching so that they could make sure they had a class with me. I think in a few cases I was like the mom they wished they had, but in most they just felt respected and enjoyed for who they were. And as they grew up, who they were became more and more fun and enjoyable.

Some of them just ran out of classes I taught that they could take and so were my student aides in their senior year. I had four to five student aides in my very nice office in the video studio the last two years, just hanging out and very occasionally grading papers or making copies for me, both of which the school put a stop to, the grading and entering of grades in the computer stopped to preserve the anonymity of failing students and the copying because they didn't want students in the copy room where the teachers went to stand in line and wait for one of two copiers for the whole school.

Without grading or making copies, there really wasn't much a student aide could do. They just hung out, at that point looking like a bunch of college kids between classes. I just loved having them around. When they graduated, I felt like I should, too. "Well, my work here is done."

Turned out it was.

{ 12 }

# Always On

Early on in my teaching career, I learned how public perception would now make decisions for me about what I did in my spare time. Toward the end of the first semester the other speech teacher, a very young woman who was a lot of fun to be around, smart and funny in that debate team way— witty and sharp-tongued—turned out to like playing pool as much as I did. We met at one of the few places where you could play pool in Williamson County, which was of course a bar. We were having a great time—that is, I was winning—when someone noticed smoke coming from an outlet that was overloaded with Christmas lights strung throughout the place.

They began to evacuate the building but I hung back, trying to get every last shot I could. I just knew this was a minor problem, they would put it out, and we would be able to resume our game shortly.

While we were out in the parking lot waiting, Ellen looked at me suddenly and said, "We've got to get out of here! If there's a fire, there could be cameras and news reporters, and it would be bad if we were standing in this parking lot!" It could have had something to do with the fact that the local gentlemen's club shared the parking lot. This was still a small and very provincial town, even though it butted up to a large, fairly sophisticated one, and a fire in a bar was definitely on the local news radar screen.

I was stunned. I had to agree that it probably wouldn't look good, but was so sorry that I had to make a decision on what to do not by what the truth was, but by how it might look to some people who were not like me. Because I wouldn't care if a teacher did go out and shoot a game of pool in a bar, or even go to a stripper bar. They are people (teachers) (strippers, too) and deserve some time to do what they want just like the rest of us. And as long as it isn't hurting anyone, they should be able to do what they want. But that's not the way it is. Ellen was right, and as a teacher you could lose your job over something like being seen in an adult situation. Even just being accused of something and *not* having it proven can end your career.

For example, here is a close brush with a possible career-ending rumor: We had an extremely bright young man in the debate department. Kind of a loner, thin with a large curly mop of brown hair, and really excessively smart. One of those kids you just knew were going to end up on scholarship at an Ivy League school. Every time he debated (Lincoln Douglas style), he won. His points were so creative and well supported that the other debater never saw it coming, could not have prepared. He had also been in my

Poetry class, and was a damn fine writer, of course, but that's how I knew him as well as I did. Only problem was, he lived with his mom and she suffered from severe depression, the kind that makes you unable to get off the couch, the kind that makes you do un-understandable things to your kid. Not physical abuse, but capricious neglect. She decided that he could not attend the debate tournament one weekend. Just couldn't, she needed him. It was important to Galen for points overall, and it was always important for us for him to participate, so we kept asking him. Suddenly, the day of an important local tournament, and about an hour before we were scheduled to leave, she called him and told him that he could go.

Great!! Wait!! He has to have a suit!!

I was on my planning period, so we jumped in my car and drove to his house nearby to pick up the suit. We were gone maybe 15 minutes. We went to the tournament, everything went great. Good triumphed over evil.

The following week, one of the assistant principals pulled me aside and said, "I understand you put a male student in your car last week." I said yes, and explained what had happened. The assistant principal knew the student and his situation, too. But he said, "Don't EVER do that again. I know you were just doing what you thought you had to do to get the job done, but you should have had another person in the car with you at least. If someone said anything about you making a sexual advance toward that student, and it's quite possible with his mother that she would do that, your career would be over, true or not."

And he was right. As a teacher, you sign over your right to the benefit of the doubt. Any doubt about your behavior is assumed guilt by the public and panic-stricken school boards who are deathly afraid of litigation. I guess I was naïve when I decided to become a teacher, and didn't realize that having drinks and playing pool in my community would raise an eyebrow, but I didn't. I assumed that when I was off-duty, I was off.

There should be some mention of this in the education curriculum in college, this restriction in behavior and compulsion to adopt the social mores of everyone in the community or at least the most prudish members of the community. Beware.

# { 13 }

# Curriculum: Comm Apps

This is my favorite class to teach, and I could be happy teaching it the rest of my life. Speech Communications, and its mandatory place in the curriculum, came about in the late 1990s when the business community went to the state legislature of Texas and said, "We're tired of hiring people who can't communicate properly with their superiors, with their coworkers, with the public. We're tired of using our time and money to train them, and we think the schools should do it."

And the legislature said, "OK!" and promptly made Communication Applications mandatory. Since there was no particular curriculum yet, initially many types of classes would meet the requirement if they had any oral presentation component. There were even Agriculture classes in west Texas that counted, and should have, I guess, since they taught students how to present their ranching and farming projects in competition.

So, I'm raring to go as a new teacher with absolutely no idea of what Speech Communications *is*. There was no mandatory textbook, although there was one set of texts that the speech teachers had been using when the class was just about Public Speaking, not the larger concept of Communications. The other speech teacher had only been teaching one year, but her mother had taught for many years at the original high school in the district. Each of them had a formidable speech team for competition established. They had notebooks full of exercises and activities. But the freedom of that beginning was that in Communications, we could cobble together our own curriculum. That was also the danger, of course, but what we came up with definitely worked.

Speech, prior to the birth of Speech Communications, was Public Speaking. The department offered additional Speech classes to train students who wished to go further than their class requirements to compete against other high schools in Texas in events such as Lincoln-Douglas debate, which is the kind most people think of as debate. Lincoln-Douglas has two debaters at two lecterns who make a case for or against a precept of some kind and eloquently argue against each other's points, with scoring done by non-competing teachers and other members of the community.

Cross Examination Debate is relatively new, within the last twenty years, and is done in singles and doubles formats. I hated Cross Ex. It had become, in Texas, a research exercise in which each side simply read into the record all that they had, so the speech became faster and faster until it was nearly unintelligible and you wondered what on earth this skill could be used for later. I couldn't understand them half the time and refused to judge it.

There were also competitive events in Oral Interpretation, mostly acting parts of monologues from plays, and competitions for extemporaneous speechwriting and delivery, in which the student was provided with a current political topic and had to write and deliver a five-minute speech within about twenty minutes. For this event, the students brought along 3-5 fileboxes of current event research, or as many as space on the bus would allow and they could manage once there. They carried these "extemp boxes" around strapped on two wheeled dollies.

Although I was hired simply to teach the general population a mandatory communications class, I was a part of the Speech Department and was expected to support it in some way. I never taught any of the debate classes, which would be considered Speech II and III and so on—never wanted to—but I did get to know the kids on the teams and go to tournaments with them. I got a thrill of pride seeing the kids at those tournaments. They were all dressed up, boys in their suits, girls in their suits and high heels and stockings, looking like a bunch of excited, really young lawyers. I also coached the Oral Interp kids in basic monologues from plays and novels since I had a theatre background.

I do like to cook (that coming-to-adulthood thing in New Orleans), so I volunteered to run the kitchen/coaches' lounge when we hosted a tournament at our high school in my fourth year. This meant feeding a hundred teachers from competing schools dinner, breakfast, lunch, dinner and breakfast over a weekend and wowing them so that they would make sure to pick our tournament every year as one of the ones they attended. Many of these seriously competitive departments came from across the state and were staying in local hotels. So the adults were trapped at our school without cars, dependent on the bus for their transportation.

I had been to a few of the local tournaments and it wasn't hard to one-up the competition in the kitchen. I set out real cream for their coffee instead of that horrid powder, in little ice bowls to keep it fresh. Coffee is very important when some of these competitions last way into Saturday night. I put local newspapers on each of the ten tables we had as our 'diner'. There were jigsaw puzzles and a computer set up to check their email.

And the food! Turkey sausage gumbo, Cuban black-bean soup, red beans and rice, tarragon pasta salad with aioli, cole slaw with blue cheese, breakfast casseroles, bread pudding, and on and on. And I did all of it on $400. (Tell me I'm going to feed a hundred people, and I'm thinking beans, rice and pasta.) Tournaments are a great money-maker for the Speech Department, from the fees for the students to participate. Those funds went to pay for our department's students to attend other tournaments.

That week of cooking was fun, fun, fun. I took all of my speech classes into the Home Ec department to get it done. They either helped, studied for other classes, or played cards and stayed out of our way if they didn't cook. Some pitched in and bussed tables and helped me in the kitchen over the weekend, many of them seeing a side of school they'd never considered—competitions for smartness.

Hmmmm. It was great fun. Best of all, one of my students found his vocation there and is now a successful chef.

At the beginning of the year, the speech teachers got together and talked about what they thought would make a good curriculum and would satisfy the intent of the recent legislation. Since I was the new kid, they brought me under their wing and gave me notebooks of activities, assignments, and quizzes. But for me, there had to be a theme or an arc to the whole curriculum that would make sense to me so I could make it make sense to anyone else. So I came up with what I called an organic structure. It went from inside to outside and grew in a logical order. Here's what I mean: we start with communication with self, then go outside to communication with another person, then to a small group, then to a large group. Throughout this arc, we still had to fulfill the old requirements of public speaking, so I usually used oral methods of assessing understanding of these types of communication.

We started the year with a couple of tried-and-true speeches. The first is the Introductory speech in which the speaker introduces another student. Then they switch. This allows each student to get up in front of the group for the first time but not alone. They can't chicken out, because the other person needs them to complete the assignment, and they feel much calmer being with someone else. They have to choose someone they don't know, so the task often illustrates for them how one could go about getting to know someone instead of the normal method of hearing what the person is like through the grapevine and forming an opinion without actually ever coming into contact with the person. I always pointed out that we are all more alike than we are different, and they were usually delighted to find that they had something in common with the new person. Some made friendships that still exist today.

Building a community of people is very important. Class has to be a safe place to get up in front of other people and do something you were scared to death to do. That's not an exaggeration; studies have shown that many people are more afraid of public speaking than death. The start of getting someone over that is letting them see that the other people in the class are like them and rooting for them, not unlike them and looking to pick them apart.

The second speech was the How-To speech. This teaches the basic framework of a speech, the old "Tell em what you're gonna tell 'em—then you tell 'em—then tell 'em what you told 'em," or: introduction, body and conclusion. The point of the speech is not to actually teach the audience something, just to demonstrate that you know the difference between intro, body, and conclusion. I told them to pick something they had done a lot, boil it down to 3-5 steps, and put those on an index card. Then write an introduction on the other side of the card, "Today I'm going to show you how to make Kool-Aid using water, sugar, a pitcher and a spoon, and any flavor of Kool-Aid you want." Write at the end of the steps "Conclusion," and then go back and repeat the intro, of course changing it from "I'm going to show you" to "Now I've shown you." The Most Basic Speech.

Of course, some people did want to show off their weird hobby, like some type of model-building or origami, which had never crossed paths with school before, and the rest of us were appropriately wowed. But my favorites were the really simple ones, like "How to Make Kool-Aid," in which I learned:

1. Never inhale after you have poured the Kool-Aid powder into the pitcher.

2. The favorite flavor of all black people is red, even though there are at least seven red flavors.

Or "How to Use Q-Tips." "See, it says right here on the box: Do not put inside ear canal. Now take the Q-tip in your thumb and index finger, place it in your ear canal like so, and swirl it—Ahhhhhhhh." "How to Open a Chip Bag," which taught me to pull the seam in the back. As extra credit, two of my students did a hilarious version of "How to Make a Sandwich" with one guy standing behind the other guy and threading his arms through the front guy's clasped hands in the back, so that you are looking at one person but another person's arms and hands are making the gestures. The one in front, one of my favorite students all four years, was a big and brawny football player, so the gestures made by the student behind who was one of the most wickedly funny people I have ever known, sometimes went to the effeminate drag queen sort and we could barely breathe we were HAHAHAing so hard. And I got paid for that!

## { 14 }

# Intrapersonal: Who are You?

After getting a couple of speeches under our belts, it was time to get into the Communications aspect of the class. The "communication with self" I mentioned before is also called "intrapersonal communication" and the way I taught it was to have the students begin by completing a personality profile. This is an assessment in which the student chooses one of four answers to questions about themselves. They must choose only one, even when none or more than one apply, so they have to spend enough time with each question to distinguish the small differences that make one answer only slightly better than another.

This type of personality analysis has been used by humans for centuries; the ancient Greeks divided people into four basic groups that were called Sanguine,

Melancholy, Choleric, and Phlegmatic. Myers and Briggs created an instrument that divides people into the same four groups but then into four subtypes each, so there are sixteen possibilities, based on the work of Carl Jung. The types are combinations of two types of perception, extroverted and introverted, and two types of judgment, logical and intuitive. For these kids, 16-17 years old, who had never even thought that there was anyone in the world like them, four was enough. I was given a batch of materials for an assessment that placed people in one of four animal types: lion, otter, beaver, and golden retriever. This was great for kids, so that they had a visual emblem as well.

The first class was taken up with explaining what a personality assessment was, handing it out and having them take and score it themselves. I explained what the four animal types represented, and had them get into groups of their animal. At this point, they only had a half hour left of class. I handed them a big sheet of butcher paper and markers, and told them to present something to the class on their 'type'. Then I observed them and the results were always the same: the lions didn't get anything done because they were all trying to be the leader and get their idea heard, the otters didn't get anything done because they were too busy laughing and saying, "Oh! You're an otter? I'm an otter, too! Do you think it's true? I think my boyfriend, mom, whatever is a retriever. Isn't this amazing?"

The beavers would always send an emissary to me, "Miss, do you have a *dictionary* or something with a *picture* of a beaver so we can get it right?" And the golden retrievers were busy telling the one retriever with a marker who had drawn or lettered anything on the paper, "Oh, you're *good*! You're really good! Do you take art lessons or something?" No one ever got to the point of presenting, the time was too short for them to make it. I stopped them with five minutes left and told them what I had just watched and that they were the same every time in all my classes.

The point of the lesson is that when you have a group composed of people just like you, your weaknesses overwhelm your strengths. You need to have a mix of people for an effective team, so you can take advantage of all the different strengths. I handed out index cards and had the students put their names and their personality types on them for me, and I used them for composing groups later in the year.

The assessment for understanding what they had just learned was a short speech in which they described what they thought of their animal type, did they agree or disagree, and did they see any of the other animal types in their lives? I had given them the basic characteristics for all four animals, with more in-depth strengths and weaknesses for their own type. The speeches were delivered over the next week.

We had people talking about understanding their mom or dad for the first time, their boyfriend, etc, people who had laboriously retyped the assessment so they could give it to someone they knew, real glimpses of understanding and of relief that they were not weird, that there were other people just like them. The funniest were the ones who told me privately that the strength characteristics were extremely accurate, but the weaknesses they just didn't have. I laughed and let them know that they had both, or the tendencies for both, and just to keep an eye out for them. It was a genuine honor to introduce these people to themselves in this way at this time in their lives.

{ 15 }

# Interpersonal with One Person: Job Fair

To move out on the arc, from intrapersonal to interpersonal, I used the job interview. I figured that would demonstrate compliance with the state mandate of the course, because this was really what the business community had in mind when they made the class compulsory. The activity took three weeks to run.

First, I picked six students from each class that I could send to the library on their own to complete something. Four of them became company representatives who would be looking to fill several job openings at a Job Fair. Two became college reps with scholarships to offer. A presentation in front of the class was required, in which they described the company, the jobs they were looking to fill, and presented their logo on a poster. The school reps had to describe their school, their campus and the scholarships available, which had to include academic, sports, and community service, plus the academic and sports had to require community service as part of their eligibility. A school insignia and poster was also required. While these six students were working in the library, the rest of us were working on resumes and job applications. One of the requirements for the week was to bring in a blank job application. All this required was going into a business and asking for one. I coached them on what not to wear, what to say. Twice I had students say that the manager asked them if they wanted an interview right then; one kid had a job offer just for asking for an application! It was a boom time in Austin, before the 2001 high-tech dot-com crash, and there were signs out everywhere that help was wanted. The kids even asked me what the point of this unit was, when it was so easy to get a job. I explained that it wouldn't always be this way, and the jobs they really wanted would be harder to get than the entry-level jobs. When they brought back the applications, we made a notebook of them as a reference resource, then made a generic application for our class project. They had to fill out three of them, plus have a resume, for their three interviews, two for jobs and one for a school.

The resumes were written in the computer lab. It was one of the few times I could figure out how to use technology for this class, other than recording speeches. Teachers are evaluated on how well they integrate technology into a class, and that's good, but it's very difficult to take a class to a computer lab. The control part is nearly impossible: there are thirty of them, one of you, they are all thirty engaged in separate activities, only some of them what you want, and you have to direct them to a point where you can have something accomplished and leave. They want to get on the internet (and this was before facebook), they want to jump ahead, they are stuck and can't catch up, their computer is frozen. It's a nightmare. When the chaos got out of hand, I would yell, "Alright! I'm going to turn this van around and we can just go home!" which was their humorous notice that the teacher had had enough and they needed to focus on what I wanted right then.

The resume we used was based on a simple template in Microsoft Word, but I had to lead them along in appropriate entries and eliminating headings that didn't apply to them, like Experience. When it came to Education, they needed to enter the name of our high school and their expected year of graduation. Under the Activities/Hobbies heading, I explained that it was almost more important simply that they have a hobby than what it is—because employers want a well-rounded individual—but playing video games is probably not a good one. I taught them how to write the purpose statement at the beginning: "Seeking a customer service position in a progressive retail organization." I told them that in this case, it was okay to start sentences with verbs, especially when they described any experience they had. Leave out the "I" and say "handled, served, prepared, provided, assisted." Makes you sound much busier, like you've been rushing around doing things. I made the point that community service is important and is viewed highly in job and school applications, so if they didn't have any to put on their resume, they should think about helping out somewhere next time they were complaining about being bored.

They learned about formatting with headings and bullets, fitting it all on one page, how to get a reference from someone and how to let them know you are putting them down as a reference, as well as who would be an appropriate reference. Although they didn't have to actually contact them, they did have to figure out an adult, not related, and get their contact information for our purposes. This was a big deal; they had never thought of this before and wanted to use their friends, their moms or aunties. If they didn't have a former employer, it needed to be a teacher, coach, or minister, not family.

Don't worry about the six best students, the ones who were off becoming business owners and HR people; they were with us by this time so that they could end up with a resume. I bought a hundred floppy discs a semester to give them their resume for future use and updating. Just in case you're wondering how teachers spend an average of $400 of their own money each year for class materials, there's a little example.

This computer resume section generally took three 90-minute classes to complete, and that was pushing them hard to give me a printed copy at the end. Some were not quite complete, but we had to move on and they had something in hand anyway. Next was a full-class lecture on job interviews. What types: individual, group, stress interviews. (I knew about those first-hand.) What was expected: that they communicate! So they should have some questions about the job like what did people really like about it, what did they not like? Why were they hiring for it, would any benefits be offered, why did the last person leave? Did the company provide any assistance with higher education for employees? I coached them to be active interviewees, not just interrogation subjects. They had to write down two questions they would ask in the mock interviews we were setting up.

I had created a rubric for scoring in the mock interviews. A rubric is a scoring sheet that lists the levels of performance for each area to be graded in a complex project. I could not be present at all the interviews at once, so the students had to score each other. I know what you're thinking here, but to eliminate unearned generosity of grading, there was a sliding scale of how much they put into the preparation and the role-playing, and also the interviewees scored the interviewers. I pre-scolded them on giving too high a score, that being discerning was part of maturity and I was asking them to show me this ability to make distinctions in behavior.

The six interviewers then gave their presentations and placed their calendars out. Wow. When you just give a smart kid a task they take it far beyond what you thought they might do. There were companies and schools that I was sure existed they were so detailed. I was always so proud of what they came up with! I had given them some resources to use like job data and scholarship listings, but they really ran with it every time.

The Job Fair would consist of ten-minute interviews, with five minutes in between. The students had to sign up for three interviews, preferably two jobs and one scholarship, over a three-day period. We had a quick lesson on handshakes, which was oddly necessary for these kids. Who is going to teach you these things? Some of them had great handshakes to begin with, but most needed a bit more gusto, and some had that awful limp handshake or the one where they just take your fingers in theirs. Yech!! It was great to have a place where someone could say to you, "Here, put the web of your hand to the web of the other person's and shake three times, looking them in the eye while you do it." Not to let them go out into the world with a wimpy handshake for years.

Then the big day came, or the big three days. I had scouted locations all over the school and placed desks and chairs for the interviews in quiet stairwells and hallway nooks. The classroom became a reception/lobby area where folks just waited for their next interview, polished up their applications, or were just generally as nervous as if they were going to a real interview. I ran from one interview location to another just spying from a distance during each interview time period to make sure they were on task and not just chatting.

And with all of the preparation, it really worked. They dressed for the interviews, some of them even bringing their nice clothes and changing between classes, because appearance was on the rubric. The interviewers definitely dressed up and looked like they really enjoyed wearing their church clothes to school for a reason. After all, they had been chosen to do this, they were proud. The interview rubrics came back with realistic scores on them, and the final piece of the activity was a sort of debriefing piece of writing in which they had to tell me what they learned. Over and over I heard that when I first described the mock interviews, they thought it was stupid, it wouldn't work, they dreaded it and hated that I was going to force them to do it. But after all of the work they put in, they were breathlessly excited that they felt like they had been through real interviews, now they knew what to do in an interview, they weren't afraid of them any more, etc, etc. I was thanked over and over for setting this up for them, and believe me I was thrilled that it worked, too. Three weeks activity, with a week of prep before it for me, was a huge investment and it paid off big time. I had students who went out and were hired during the week of the mock interviews who rushed into class the next day, "Miss! Miss! It was just like you said!" The interviewers confided that they were now thinking of owning a business when they grew up. Some kids actually went out and volunteered to get some community service they could put on their resumes.

The other speech teachers had told me that I was putting too much into it. The idea had grown out of a one-day mock interview activity that one of them had given me, and they all had in their files. The full-on setup, combined with my conviction that this was what the class was all about, this was what the legislature had in mind when they had made the class mandatory, a sort of righteousness and good-over-evil drive to it, made it work very, very well.

I created a course evaluation for the students at the end of the semester. No one was getting evaluations from students at the high school level, but every class I took in college did and now I know that every adult education class has to have student evaluations at the end. It only makes sense to hear from the actual consumer. On those student evaluations, the job interview activity was most often cited as the favorite of the year.

{ 16 }

# Interpersonal: Small Group Meetings

After intrapersonal communication with one other, I grew it bigger by moving to small groups, and taught them How to Have a Productive Meeting. At the beginning of each semester, there is a Back to School Night, when parents are invited to the campus to meet their student's teachers for the semester. They go through their child's schedule, bells ringing and all, and spend ten minutes in each class. The teacher tells them what will be taught in that class and encourages them to sign up on the sheet with their contact information since it takes an act of Congress to get it from a student's file in the counselor's office (they don't hear that part, but that's why).

I always told them about my arc theory of curriculum delivery, and what I used to teach the stages of communication with self, communication with one other, communication with a small group, and communication with a large group. The example I used for small group was "How many of you have been in a meeting where you wished you were back at your desk so that you could actually get something done?" All hands went up. "Well, I'm going to teach your kids how to have a productive, short meeting whether they are the leader or a member." At this point, their hands would go back up, "Can we come?"

By this point, I had student buy-in. After the job interview activity, they knew that I would set activities up so that they would work, so I had a lot less convincing to do. I put them into groups according to what their personality type had been before—lion, otter, beaver, or golden retriever—with a blend of types in each group. I admonished the lions to not always assume the leadership role just because no one else would volunteer right away.

We started with group dynamics, what a group leader is and is not, how the leader's opinions or ideas don't count any more than the others', it's just their job to make sure everyone is heard and the meeting ends on time. How to handle different stumbling blocks, like folks who won't talk, ones who wait for the boss to talk before getting off the fence and joining him/her (brown-nosers), people who dominate the meeting and waste everyone's time talking about themselves and not moving towards the goal at all (make them the scribe to take notes, that'll keep 'em busy). The importance of true brainstorming, how important it is to hear everyone's ideas, even the crazy ones, because even if it's crazy and there's no way we could do it, hearing it may spark a doable one in someone else, or allow someone with vision to combine two crazy undoable ideas into one that just. might. work. I convinced them that it is a truism of life that more heads are better than one, that without a lot of input you end up with a poverty of ideas. Sometimes high-schoolers, especially smart ones, think they know it all and how could that dork possibly have anything to contribute. Getting them past this is often the main thing they learn in this section.

I would tell them that I was like them, even as an adult, until I *had* to make sure to hear from the quiet ones in all types of classes and often found that they had the most insight. And here I thought they were just passively overwhelmed by our brilliance, the talky ones. For our purposes, we adopted the policy of "No one speaks twice until everyone speaks once." Drives them crazy but makes them seek that input from the quiet kids, at least so that they can have another turn themselves.

I taught them a simple 5-step meeting process:

1. Define the problem, the purpose of the meeting. Write it down. This is so that later, when people want to lead the meeting down a trail to nowhere, people can point to it and say, "That's something we need to fix, too, but this is what we agreed to focus on in this meeting."

2. Define the criteria for the solution, what the answer would look like, as in "It has to do this and this, it cannot

do this." "It has to cost less than budget and cannot take more than two weeks to do." "The choice has to keep the minister a part of the church but get him out of the pulpit." Prioritize the criteria: this is very important, and will eliminate fights later if you can prioritize the criteria before they have someone's idea attached to them.

3. Brainstorm solutions. Have ideas as fast as you can and dump them onto the scribe's pad. Make sure you set up an atmosphere and an expectation in which nothing is too crazy: explain to the members that you want all of the ideas--even the crazy ones because even if we don't choose the crazy one because it's, well, crazy, it may inspire the best idea in someone else's brain just hearing it, or get combined with another idea, like, "No, we can't do that, but if we use Brittany's idea and add that to it, it could work."

4. Choose one of the solutions. Go back to the criteria and apply them in priority order to the possible solutions to make a decision everyone agrees with, or at least most people agree with. The group has consensus.

A word here about consensus: Many people believe that consensus means most everyone, some people even think it must even be unanimity. Consensus simply means one more than half. It is the same as simple majority. When used as a method of decision-making for a group, however, 'consensus' expresses the idea that everyone has had a part in the process, rather than simply voting 'yay' or 'nay' on one person's ideas. By teaching the students this method of working in small groups, we hope to increase consensus, that feeling that you have been heard and considered, across the spectrum of meetings: business meetings, school board meetings, church board meetings, scout troop meetings, all meetings.

    5. Finally, ACT. So often meetings end with a decision made but no action is taken right away. Once the solution is chosen, the steps to complete it should be broken down and assigned to people in the group for completion, and get their agreement right then and there that they understand it's their job and they will do it.

After this method was explained, we used it to complete several old case-study type problems. One was: "You are a team on a hospital and have one heart for transplant. The following ten people need transplants. Choose which one gets the heart." There's an old priest, a young boy with autism, a guy with possible Mafia ties but who has sponsored dozens of needy kids, a woman with children and a disabled husband, a very wide range. It's a great exercise to teach kids about making adult decisions and how to recognize good criteria for a solution. Basically, they have to choose by prioritizing the criteria before they apply them to each possible solution (the people who need the transplants are the possible solutions). This problem can even be solved mathematically, and if we had time I showed them that method. Sometimes it puts their mind at ease that in a gut-wrenching situation, they made the absolute best decision, since it was a couple of decimal points higher than the other one.

Another case study has to do with a minister for a church. "You are the Board of Directors, and must make a decision about what to do with the minister. He has begun to wander in his sermons and the church is losing steam and members because of it. However, this minister has grown this church from a very small denomination to a pretty large one. There is a parsonage on the property and there are two junior ministers that function well in the church. You have to come up with a plan and figure out who is going to tell the minister and how. And what if he doesn't like the idea, what if this, what if that..." This exercise opens up the brainstorming and assignment of actions parts.

There are several others to choose from, most all speech teachers and some English teachers have these old activities in their files. The students loved them and felt grownup by the decisions they were making, even though it was just role-playing. The assessment for each of them was a rubric created so that the kids assessed themselves and the group they were a part of *while* they were in the meeting. Did everyone take part, was disagreement channeled back into the process, etc. Since they were all graded on whether everyone contributed, they made sure that everyone did. What did they notice about the personality types in the group, and did it function well or poorly because of the mix? The assessment for the unit was an average of their self-assessments for the activities and a written piece on the whole thing. These written pieces were free form, I really just wanted to hear from each of them what they found valuable, what they thought didn't work, how they thought they could use this in real life. I generally graded very liberally on this part, by length of response. A half page was a C, a page was a B, and anything over a page was an A. It made them not worry so much about structure and just tell me what they thought. And the more they told me, the better the grade.

{ 17 }

# Large Group: Student Congress

The class ended with Communication in a Large Group. The way I taught this was by teaching Parliamentary Procedure. I staged a Student Congress in each class the last two weeks of every semester. It was great for me—while all of the other teachers were scurrying around in the copy-room and grading final exams, I was sitting in the back of the room assessing how well the students debated their bills and resolutions. This also counted as their Persuasive Speech.

The unit started with learning what bills and resolutions are, then drafting an idea or two about what they would like to do. I told them that it could apply to our school, city, state, country, world, or galaxy. No one ever did any galaxy ones. I was a bit disappointed. Maybe that was my generation, with Star Wars and Star Trek. I taught about change, how these were meant to signal change (resolution) or start change happening (bill). A bill is a piece of legislation that becomes a law. A resolution is a statement of belief that you want the body to subscribe to.

One of my very favorite parts of teaching was getting revenge upon the students who had been a constant drag on the rest of the class. Generally, they were boys who were wasting their time and everyone else's with wiseass comments having to do with the stupidity of school, how cool they were personally, drug references, sexual innuendo, and how useless these activities were. They took up way too much of my time and I resented it.

In the beginning of my teaching career, I vowed that no one would sleep in my class. I thought it was unconscionable, when I saw seasoned teachers allowing it. I would walk by and gently touch the sleeper on the arm, they would raise their head grouchily and look at me as though I were insane. All the while I would be announcing, "Nobody sleeps in my class!" I had something important to give them and they had to stay awake to get it. As time went on I discovered that these guys didn't value school or my class so they thought it was okay to sleep and I let them. It gave the rest of us a chance to move on more quickly. The only problem comes when they flunk. More about that later, but for now let me tell you about the real learning experience for them in Student Congress.

Often, these deadbeats would come to me and confide, "Miss, I can't do this. I don't know anything to write on." This was because they were asleep when I was giving examples. So I would re-suggest a few of the deadbeat hall of famers. "How about ending mandatory school after eighth grade? Not all countries have twelve grades of school, and in the majority of states you can quit at age sixteen. I could help you with the research on that one. I've done a bit myself so I could even be a source. Or how about ending the no pass-no play rule at school?" They always took the bait.

I really do believe that ending compulsory high school education would solve a lot of our problems. Let it suffice to say that it was a beautiful thing to watch when these guys puzzled through the concept during research, saying, "Hey, wait a minute, that means that in eighth grade we take a test to see if we stay in school or not? I don't think you're old enough to take anything seriously in eighth grade, Miss..." meaning *they* didn't, and they were starting to get the fear of loss of the guaranteed education. But they were into it now, so they would end up in front of the class talking about how yeah, this was a great idea. Maybe by this time they didn't think it was great, but still pretty good. I loved the look of utter surprise on their faces when NO ONE in the class would debate the other side and the other kids told them to their face that "We would rather you weren't here, you take up so much of the teacher's time, we would rather be able to go faster in the class." Here they had been thinking all along that the rest of the class was totally behind them, just waiting for their next amazingly witty comment, thinking that they were so cool to strut around and say school was a pain in the ass. And the no pass-no play guys? Priceless. They thought they were admired for their basketball or football prowess, that the rest of the students were so sorry about the unfairness, the loss, that this great potential (possibly national!) wasn't allowed to play for the school team because of a failed class. The look on their faces when the students told them that no, they didn't believe that school dollars paid by their parents' taxes should be used to provide free football gear, coaches, and a stadium to someone who couldn't (wouldn't make the effort to) even make a C in each of their classes.

This was life learning for these boys. I may seem harsh, and every semester I started out empathetic and really worked with them, but you have to understand that this was at the end of the semester. They had worn me out and they had it coming. I just set them up. But they did learn something vital. That everyone didn't think like they did, that they were not the darling class clown they thought they were, that other kids really did want to learn and found school valuable, and if they did then they had better refocus.

Student Congress wasn't just about revenge, though. It was a great way to teach how to communicate in a large group while showing how government works. We had bills on gun control, abortion, alternative fuels, locker privacy, cell phone use in schools, and other issues the students really cared about, and resolutions that the US should make changes in education, foreign policy, environmental issues. They had to do research in the computer lab to cite at least two real sources in their written piece. I taught them the simple format for drafting their document, then taught them the basics of Parliamentary Procedure and the most basic of Roberts' Rules of Order: motions, seconds, tabling, referring to committee, recesses and adjournments. I required that they have someone ready to debate the other side, then open for other debate. Every class was amazed when I opened the session, turned the gavel over to them and went to the back of the room as one of the participants. They usually came up with the idea that they could recess and be done early for the day, but I let them know that although they could certainly do that, they couldn't finally adjourn until all legislation had been debated and voted upon. If we didn't get through everyone's bill or resolution, we would be there after school ended for everyone else since it was a final grade. The next day they would get down to business. We generally got through four pieces of legislation per day per class. At the end of the eight days of congress, they would adjourn the session and then had to write a piece on what they had learned, in addition to a short multiple-choice test on the terms.

Sometimes they would tell me that they didn't think anyone would speak against their bill because of course they would all be for it. I let them know that they didn't have to believe it—they just had to debate it, like an attorney who doesn't really believe that his client is innocent but defends him because that's what he's paid to do and he believes in the process. I taught them that much of what goes on in Congress happens in the halls, when you get your buddy to help you out by voting for your bill if you'll vote for his, or in our case by agreeing to debate against yours if you will fulfill that role for him. There were a lot of 'Aha!'s in that class, and some kids decided that politics might be a good career choice once they understood the format. I had several kids tell me they thought they would go into law as a result of Student Congress.

## { 18 }

# Poetry

Since I refused to teach freshman English again after the first semester, they gave me Poetry. Actually, I don't think that my refusal had anything to do with it. If they needed me to teach freshman English again that would have been the class, but I was lucky enough to get Poetry, which was considered an elective. There are very few electives left. When kids are told that they will need an elective to fill in the hours on a schedule, there are really very few classes that would qualify, that are not English or Science or Spanish. There's art, band, and theatre, and that's about it at most schools. Just no money for those 'extra' classes. This is another part of how we are letting kids down by not providing them with a trade that doesn't require college.

Somehow, I got to teach the classes most like electives. Poetry the first year, Multi-media the second, and Video Technology starting the third year. What this meant was that I had an odd assortment of students in those classes. There were some students who genuinely wanted to take that class, mixed with students who just needed the hours of an elective and this was the least onerous. In the poetry class I ended up with some of my favorite kids who came from both groups, the ones who made the biggest impression on me, or was it because we were writing poetry and I saw them for who they really, really were?

Many teachers hate to teach poetry, and I think it's because they don't enjoy poetry in the first place. They don't read it, they don't write it. I love poetry, and it has been a part of my life and library for all my life, so I was happy to try it. Believe me, it's not hard to teach teenagers about poetry. They are living their lives on the bleeding edge already. To give them permission, nay to force them to think in dramatic terms, to find expressions that are visceral for the reader, is like telling the Tar Baby you're going to put him in the Briar Patch. (Oh, no! Not the Briar Patch!!)

This class was just called Poetry, not Reading Poetry or Writing Poetry, so I decided we would be writing it. I did read to them every day, a favorite poem of mine introducing them to poets like Whitman or Dickinson or Rumi, the 13th-century Sufi poet who wrote incredibly passionate passages about his relationship with God. But mostly I taught them about poetic tools like metaphor, repetition and alliteration, and we wrote.

In the beginning, there is some grousing by the large football player types, and some whining by the videogamers that they can't think of what to write. But the key to teaching people how to write poetry is to put them in a box. Give them a task to perform while writing the poem and their brain really starts to work. If you tell someone to just write a poem, it's very hard to do. But if you tell them to write a poem and take away their choice in several areas, like subject, format, or length, then it becomes a problem to solve and uses different parts of the brain. They are suddenly engaged, because people like to solve problems even more than they like to create. So, we had to write in iambic pentameter, or in a sonnet format, or as a recipe with ingredients and steps, or as a letter. We did haikus out the wazu. I loved the class. I wrote with them. Some of mine were better, some theirs. I found out about a local poetry contest and they all had to enter as an assignment; several won and we all went downtown for a public reading and to pick up their awards on a Saturday afternoon.

You may ask what the relevance of poetry is today. The students I taught would tell you that it taught them to think about words more carefully. It gave them an appreciation of an art form they had not, or thought they had not, encountered before. An art form they could participate in, not only by reading others' poems or enjoying the lyrics of a song, but by writing poems and lyrics themselves.

And there were some very good writers in there. There were some poems written that haunt me still, and some kids who could write in a way that captured what had gone wrong with the lives of many others like them. Because even though this school was diverse, and the students I knew were funny and smart, there were those whom other adults would consider scary. Kids who suffered from abuse, kids who suffered from neglect (which I think is in many ways an abuse that is even worse than physical or emotional abuse). Here are a few of the poems from the literary magazine that we published that speak about those adults:

### Sittin' in My Room

Sittin' in my room with not a care at all
Not worrying about friends not even the mall
Playing games that made youngsters chuckle and laugh
Wonder why each day in the hood go by so fast

Acting bad with no thoughts in my brain
Playing football getting hurt and including new stains
My biggest role model was so easy to see
It was my favorite uncle, my Uncle O.T.

Getting wrote up every day at my school
Hoping Momma wasn't gonna kill me for acting a fool
Hoping I'd grow up to be handsome and tall
Just sittin' in my room with not a care at all

But now Uncle O.T. done got locked up
And little Bam Bam ain't a little boy, he's all grown up
Talking to girls has replaced most of my free time
Combined with sleepin' and Al Green to relieve my mind
My role model remains my Uncle O.T.
That'll never change cause he was so special to me
Life for me ain't changed that much
Except for getting a job from the school job program, it really sucked

So like a flower my life still has to bloom
I'm just sittin' here, sittin' here in my room
—Samuel Warner

## The Infamous Barrel

The boy awakens
Rises from his bed
And runs to the corner of his room
To where his toy box is and pulls out
The Barrel
The Barrel of monkeys
The boy dumps the barrel out onto the floor
Mixes them up
And just stares
He has no friends
His parents have basically
Forgotten him
And there is no brother
Or even a sister to play with
The monkeys are his friends
All twelve of them
He found the Barrel, so some are missing
But he doesn't care
Now he has someone to talk to
Spike—the light green one—he likes to pick his nose
Buddy—the blue one—he just sleeps
Penny—the orange one—she is a giggler
Max—the white one—he is afraid of loud noises
Sunshine-the yellow one-she just smiles a lot...a lot
Tiana—the purple one—she is a hugger
Butch—the black one—he is kind of a bully
Debra—the brown one—she loves poetry
Jimmy-the gray one-he likes to play hide and seek
Karl—the dark green one—likes Penny
Kris—the blue-green one—is a fighter

He never actually starts a fight
But he likes to play around
And then there is Kabal
When the boy found the Barrel
Kabal seemed to have been burned
Over half of its left arm was gone
And the foot on the left was frayed
It seemed to have been chewed on
Because there were small indentions all over it
And it was burned
Body and face twisted and deformed
From what could only be described as
Caused by fire
Kabal was the boy's favorite
He could relate to him the most
Every monkey
Spike-Buddy-Penny-Max
Sunshine-Butch-Tiana-Debra
Jimmy-Karl-Kris
Was a reflection of himself
But Kabal was the one that he really liked
And so every day
In the confinements of his room
The boy would dump out The Barrel
The Barrel of Monkeys
And play
Play with his only friends
Why. Why must it be like that you say.
Why don't you ask the boy
I'm right here
—Elijah Stamps

After a lesson on how repetition of a word or phrase gives it more and more power each time, Jacob Payne wrote a piece about the central Texas weather:

Heat

With these hot days
Now hundred hits
With sweltering heat
In this southern home

Now hundred hits
My heart beating fast
In this southern home
My breath at sigh

My heart beating fast
No wind to chill
My breath at sigh
Why do I live

With sweltering heat
No wind to chill
Why do I live
With these hot days
—Jacob Payne

(A note about Jacob: He was a paraplegic with MS, and by the time I knew him, he could no longer speak. Many of his classmates had known him as a normal boy when they were kids. Many did not, so only knew him as the kid in the wheelchair. He was brilliant, and it was so poignant to read his poetry, which never referred to his disease or current physical state. Jacob passed away last year.)

I told them to find poets they liked and imitate them, get into their rhythm and use of words, and it would rub off and make them a better poet. Here is one:

Dreams of a Dream
Scrawlings of a lyrical night mumm'rd I listen,
Controversial tongues of silence, trivial choirs,
Pyros delicately remembering, periodical drafts levitated texture and long,
Droplets of unseen veins, rivers of an island conversing, forever conversing,
(Or is it the clashing of lips? The mourningless blood of human lips?)
I glance, just glance heavenward, entire love masses,
Dreamfully creepily they run, cowardly drawing and erasing,
With at times an un-light'd, dread'd blocked off spark,
Appearing and disappearing.

(some birth rather, some saddened uninhibited birth;
on the prairies to souls inconceivable,
Some presence is prancing over.)
[inspired by Walt Whitman]
—Chelsea Scully

And the recipe assignment yielded some excellent pieces. My favorite:

Recipe for a New Future

Requires:
One gas oven
A Magic Marker
A book of Matches
A history

Ingredients:
At least one demolished friendship or love interest
Considerable Miscommunication
Words, badly broken
Two cloves of Guilt
Three tablespoons of Self-Pity
Two pictures of yourself
An acceptance Letter
A car
Several hundred miles of highway
A pinch of purpose
And just a hint of destiny

Preheat oven to 500, but don't forget to blow out the pilot light.

While oven is preheating call the demolished friendship or love interest and practice Considerable Miscommunication. Once that is completed, sauté the broken words with the

Two Cloves of Guilt. Add Self-Pity before Guilt begins to brown. Cover and allow to settle. Meanwhile prepare the pictures of yourself by scribbling a cryptic note on their backs with the Magic Marker. Season to taste.

When finished set the two pictures beside the acceptance letter. Contemplate history then return to Guilt mixture. Stir.
It will thicken. Just before it congeals, scoop the mixture into separate bowl You and the other Me. Crawl into the oven and place the bowls on either side of you. Wait. Begin eating from the bowl labeled Me.

When you realize what you are doing, crawl out of the oven. Break the bowls over the sink and flush mixture with copious amounts of water. Dust self with purpose and sense-of-destiny. Throw away the pictures. Get into the car, and complete recipe by placing Several hundred miles of highway between you and your History. Welcome to your new future.
—Erin Machniak

    We published a literary magazine; it was very good. The students were the jury for anonymous entries (only I knew who the poets were). They ended up selecting at least one from everyone. They were thrilled with this process, as well as the editing, the design, and even the construction (comb-bound). We sold copies at the school to cover the cost of the printing and some money for gas and lunch when the contest winners went downtown to do their readings.

I've kept up with some of them and now they are over thirty years old, some have families, one has a music production company started when he discovered his ability to rap in the poetry class (he ended up at UT, and came by to thank me!) One went to college for a technical degree, ended up admitting she was happier in liberal arts (the recipe poet) and writes poetry and music. I touched base with them to get permission for reprinting their poems here.

# { 19 }

# Video Studio

When the high school building where I taught was designed, the superintendent of the school district was a man who had been in that position for many years, initially for a small farming community. It's surprising that he was ahead of the curve in insisting that a video studio be a part of the design. It was a large space, with three small sound/editing booths off of it and a large control room with glass between that and the studio space. It was very tall, probably 25 feet, with the steel underside of the roof structure and the steel trusses exposed. It was cinderblock construction, with a linoleum floor. It was used to pathetic effect by a couple of teachers prior to me, who just put a few student desk-chairs, a television and VCR in it. There was so much bounce of sound waves in the room that you couldn't even understand that TV, much less record anything in the room. I think the previous teacher had the students watch videos about making television, or anything else the teacher could find, since he had started with one camera that was promptly stolen when he left it out.

When the principal asked me to teach video the following semester, I went to the studio to check it out. Initially, I was unimpressed to the point of not teaching it. But I really was the best one to do it, since we didn't have anyone who really knew video. I had gone to audio engineering school in the '80s and a huge part of my work experience prior to teaching was in the audio/video industry. Granted, it was more about wholesale and retail, but I did have an affinity for the equipment and I approached it as a storyteller with tools. The principal had come to think of me as the one who could figure out what to do with a weird class. I had taught the Poetry class and done well with that, the Multimedia class and figured out what to do with that, so I was a natural for the Video Technology class.

It was wide open then. Video was a newly-sanctioned class by the state, so there were no prerequisites for the students or the teacher. Now you have to have an additional certification that is very involved with the equipment. That is a little bit of a cruel joke, because for most schools the equipment is the weak point of the program due to lack of funds.

My budget was enough for one camera and one computer the first semester. I bought a Canon camera, agonizing over that vs Sony, but it was basically a very high-end consumer camera. There were a lot of young filmmakers using those cameras at the time; with that camera and iMovie on a Mac, you could make a feature film. I knew that Mac was what I wanted for video as well, did a lot of reading on the subject to determine which computer brand, and the iMovie editing software was far easier for me and for teenagers to use than any of the add-on software programs for PC. I only had eight kids the first semester, so even though it was tough with one camera and one computer for eight people, we could still make it work.

The class was to be taught in the fall semester, so over the summer I spent the rest of the budget on soundproofing the studio so that we could even stand to be in there. I sent off for a type of insulation that we installed between the steel rafters of the ceiling. Rolls of puffy insulation were unrolled and held up by wires stretched underneath the insulation between the rafters. A friend, a young man who was the technical director for the theatre department, and I completed this death-defying act using the district's cherry-picker, a machine that scissored up a platform big enough for two people with a bar around them. It had a remote control for raising and lowering the platform, so you could then drive the thing around the room. At first, you don't have your sea legs and you shake it with your nervousness, twenty feet up. After a while, we got so used to it we were driving the thing fully extended to the next position. It took us three days to get all of the insulation up, but it really did help with the sound bounce. I asked the district to carpet the room as well, which they did, so that covered two surfaces. All I had left were the walls.

I called up Walt Olden with Olden Lighting, the most well known lighting guy in Austin, and asked if he knew of any theatres replacing their curtains and he did. These are long, heavy velvet curtains and would provide pretty good sound insulation properties for the walls. I had Walt install curtain-hanging track around the entire room, and we bought those used curtains and hung them. It all worked just as I had planned.

I should mention that all of these studio upgrades were not in my budget. My budget was only $4000. The principal thought he was really giving me a lot to start a program! The average budget for an English or speech class was about $1000, so to him, he was. But when you buy a $2000 camera and a $2000 computer, you're done. All of the other upgrades, the sound insulation, the carpet, the drapes and track, were $8000 that I went to the school board and begged for. I explained why I needed them, that the room was not usable without dampening the sound, that it was a great deal because I would install the ceiling installation for free and I had found second-hand curtains for the walls. They gave me the money, less the carpeting, which they just installed for me.

The following year, I filled out a budget request form myself; I asked for $15,000, I got $8000. Still, it meant that I could buy three more cameras and three iMac computers for the sound booths. I could teach sixteen kids, and each group of four would have access to a camera and editing equipment. The first computer was the biggest Mac desktop I could get, so it had the 17" screen and a whopping SIX gigabytes of storage. This meant that it could hold six hours of video. By the time I bought the other three a year later, they each had twenty gigs of hard drive storage!

I had to fight for those Macs, too. There was a new principal by that time (Oh, woe! More later) and he did not like the idea of me using a different brand of computer than the entire school. He said I would have to use the PCs just like everyone else, because what if this class really didn't work out? And then there they would be, stuck with these Macs that no one wanted. I really had to insist that I knew what I was doing and prove that if these kids graduated and went on into video broadcast journalism as a profession or even in the university, they would be on Macs. I won, but I got an adversary.

The video studio was my only classroom. I had one video class per semester there, but I just locked up the editing booths and had three speech communications classes in there the rest of the time. This meant that the control booth became my office, which was the most fabulous office in the school. It had countertops around three sides, one under the huge window that looked out over the classroom. The big orginal computer sat on one of them. I brought in a rug, sofa, two chairs and a coffee table when I replaced our living room furniture at home. Since it was so far away from the center of the school, way down at the end of the theatre and band halls, I added a mini-fridge and small microwave for my lunches. Of course, I also had my regular teacher desk and chair and a file cabinet in there. The lighting was very cool, as it was the only place with recessed lighting in the school, and I put a dimmer switch on it just like in real control booths, so that you could have the lights only that you needed and they wouldn't spill onto the scene in the studio below. I ran a microphone and small speaker from the control booth to the studio/classroom area and vice versa, so we could communicate and so that I could hear what was going on in the studio/classroom if I was in my office (and see the students, too, of course, through the window) and could talk to them as well.

The office was such a nice space that my friend the theatre teacher and the young tech director often came to my place for lunch. We'd microwave our respective Tupperware and sit at the couch and coffee table, grateful for a homey touch that was so different it was like getting away for lunch even though we only had forty minutes.

The first semester, when I only had eight students, was heaven. These kids were some of the sharpest, wittiest people in the school and were genuinely interested in television and broadcast journalism. I laughed most of the time; they were tremendously funny in that smarty college kid way, and I think I never progressed past that much myself so I felt right at home. It was like working in a Saturday Night Live writers room. Some of them had taken their required Speech Communications class with me, some of them were new to me. We had a ball, setting up the studio, coming up with a curriculum. I made no bones about the fact that I was new to all this, too, and was just bringing them everything I could find about it, since there was no textbook. The theatre teacher and I went to a weekend video workshop at the Art Institute in Houston, at our expense of course, and picked up a lot of great material. I researched on the web for more. I cobbled together something that made sense to me, and we went with it. It certainly beat watching videos all semester.

We learned that everything is a story, from a news story to a commercial to a TV show to a feature film. We learned how to shoot the camera, entrances, exits, angles, close-ups and wide shots, special lighting, interior, exterior, storyboarding, scriptwriting, advertising, and a short history of broadcast journalism.

The second semester I had sixteen students and had to turn away kids. The next year, I was overrun with requests. I told the principal that I couldn't just take thirty kids in that class, I was only outfitted for sixteen, and I couldn't really keep an eye on all of them at once if they got into the editing booths. I got him to agree that I could limit the class to sixteen, then went to the counselors and let them know I had that approval from the principal. I also set up a prerequisite of having previously taken Speech Communications (so they would at least be juniors) and even then taking Video only with my approval. That way I could at least make sure that a spot wasn't being wasted by some deadbeat that just thought it would be a blowoff class. That's what happens with classes outside the basics, these days. As I have said before, schools don't offer any real electives, so the kids pour into anything unique and different. And the counselors are so relieved to have something that could be called an elective, they do the pouring. I did have some sway with the counselors, however, since they all had children in the school themselves and wanted me for their kid's speech teacher. So they went along with all of my demands.

The spring of that year, teachers were told that we would have an in-service day with no plan. In-service means you are working but with no students, usually something along the lines of CE, Continuing Education. There are requirements for how much in-service teachers must be subjected to. The reason I characterize it as subjugation is that it is so generalized over all curricula it is generally a joke. We had to attend a full-day in-service for 'Multiculturalism in the Classroom' once. We could have taught it. We had forty-three languages spoken in the homes of our students. It was like the UN when the bells rang. But we had to listen to an "expert from out of town" for a full day.

We had another one about the latest in brain research, which taught us you must break up your instruction into twenty minute chunks, since that's the cycle of human attention. And the first twenty minute chunk was the *most* important, from an instructional standpoint, since students were fresh after the stimulation of the halls on the way to the classroom. Then we were told that in spite of this critical new information about how people learn best, we were still required to waste the first ten minutes taking roll and sending it to the office, so that admin could get their count right as soon as possible.

For this in-service, students would be out of school for the day and we were to find something that related to our discipline to better our teaching and do it. *This was probably useful!* We could do pretty much anything as long as we didn't just catch up on grading or get copies made for the next class. We had one of these the year before, and the speech departments of both high schools got together and shared activity ideas. Now we had done that, so I told my video students that if they wanted to use their day off as well, I would try to arrange a field trip to a news station in Austin. It's impossible to go on field trips above elementary school normally, or at least hugely hassled, because the students all have four other teachers and someone of that group is not going to like letting little Jimmy out of his test. They were thrilled at the idea, so on the appointed day, we just met at the school and went down in several cars to the station.

We had a great time, and the station manager was thrilled to show off his facility to students. We finished up in the lobby where we came in, and had to wait there for my student who loved art and the graphics side. He was in the production booth in front of a Mac computer with two excited video geeks showing him what they were doing. While we were waiting for him in the lobby, the station manager asked if we had any questions.

As a matter of fact, I did. The previous day, there had been a "stabbing" at our sister high school. Actually, one special-ed kid poked another with a Bic pen. He made a scratch that did require a bandaid. With the regulations about special-ed, however, a report had to be made, so police were summoned. Some reporter listening to the police radio zoomed in on it and voila! School Stabbing!!

They broke into regular programming to broadcast the news, flipping out parents across the district who then called the school to find out if they should pick up their child, which jammed the switchboard so that no one could call in or out, so the parents rushed up to the school to become part of the melee. A reporter shoved a microphone in a student's face, and she said, "I saw blood on the floor!" which was impossible, but really enflamed the issue when broadcast on television.

Standing there in the station lobby, I asked the station manager if he knew about the previous day's story at the other high school. When he assured me he did, I asked, "When a print journalist quotes someone in a story, he/she does some fact checking for reliability of the source. What is the view of the video journalist about the source? That girl you interviewed had no actual knowledge of what was going on, and by putting her on TV, you needlessly upset parents who then *did* create a problem with traffic at the school. When you put someone on TV and they say something, don't you check to see if it's true?"

"Nah," he said, "we're not saying what she says is true, we're just saying she *said* that." The students and I just stared at him, and I could tell that they were a bit troubled by his response. Then the last student came out of the production booth and we went on our way, of course discussing this idea of no responsibility all the next day in class.

After the semester ended in June, a student called me at home and said, "Mrs. Saxon, did you notice that K—- changed their news set? Maybe we could get their old one!" I told her that yes, I had noticed and that I would give them a call, but I didn't. I didn't call because I thought that the station manager was not happy with the way that our field trip ended because of my big mouth, and I didn't want to embarrass him or myself by asking for the set.

About a week after the next semester started, the station manager called me up. He asked if I remembered him, I said of course. He asked if I noticed that they had changed their set, I said yes. He said, "I have saved that old set for your program all summer. I had it trucked up to a hangar at the Georgetown airport for storage and I will pay to have it delivered to you. How would the 11th of September be?"

I was thrilled, of course, and very grateful. I felt that he was somehow trying to make amends for so bluntly telling my students that there are no ethics in broadcast journalism, and I was happy that he wanted to do so in such a material way. The set we were using was a large wood framed semicircular countertop that was painted to look mildly okay on camera. Sort of like a theatre set, certainly not real.

On September 11th, I came in to school and walked in my office to pick up the ringing phone. It was shortly after 8am. Another teacher was calling me to let me know that a plane had crashed into the World Trade Center in New York. I turned on the little 4" TV I had in my office, saw the replay of the plane hitting the tower, thought to myself that it probably was not an accident but an attack, and then *watched* the second plane crash into the building. Now I was very frightened that we were under attack. My brother lives in New York, in the Village at that time, but was in sales so could have been anywhere.

The students started coming into class, some had seen or heard about the first crash. We turned on the big TV in the studio, which only received one local station with foil-wrapped rabbit ear antennae, and watched for the whole period. They didn't want to leave, because they would have to go to a class that might not have a TV, and they were normally checked out ahead of time by the teachers. We had ours all the time, of course.

Half of them came back with a hall pass after the next period started, to see if they could stay with me and watch what was going on. We ended up dragging the furniture out of the office to accommodate all of the students and teachers who ended up in my room to watch the horrible events unfold.

In the middle of the morning, the set was delivered. It was a beautiful, professional set with two news desks and a backdrop. Enormous truck and large men moving huge furniture into what was already a chaotic scene. Now we were scared and happy at the same time. At lunchtime, four of my best students came rushing in and said, "Mrs. Saxon! Can we use the cameras to go interview kids in the cafeteria about what's going on?"

"Absolutely! That's a great idea, man-on-the-street coverage!" I was very proud of them for taking the initiative to do this. Real broadcast journalism.

In the cafeteria, they were confronted by the new principal, who asked what they were doing and when they told him, he said they had to stop. One of my favorite and longtime students, Lisa, asked why and he angrily replied, "Because I said so!"

The girls turned to leave and Lisa said to another girl, "I just wanted to know why."

Later, the principal called me to his office. He was ready to dismantle the video program because I had the lack of control to allow students with cameras into the cafeteria to invade the privacy of other students. And he wanted to know Lisa's name, because she was a troublemaker and he wanted to suspend her. I asked what on earth she had done, and he said that she had insulted him. When she turned away in the cafeteria and said, "I just wanted to know why," to the other girl, he thought he heard her say something about his size (350 lbs) or his color (black).

First, I explained that what they were doing was called "man on the street reaction" and was a standard part of broadcast journalism, in fact he might see it on any given news show. What the students were doing was exactly what they should have been doing, being aware of the importance of what was going on around them and looking at it through the lens of how to share it with others. He asked what we intended to do with the tape, as though we would be broadcasting it raw on the school system the next day. I explained that they would probably want to edit it into a meaningful piece that may or may not go any further than my class, but that if it did they would go back to any student they included and get a video release signed. He said he just didn't like it because what if some student broke down and cried on camera because they had a loved one in New York? This was bullshit and a last ditch effort to salvage his head of steam. I replied that he needed to know that I was not an idiot nor insensitive, and that of course we would not broadcast any part that would embarrass someone. We were not there to do that, my program was not there to do that. This is an indicator of micromanagement; not trusting that a mature teacher can make a decision about what to broadcast or whether to do so at all.

I told him that Lisa was a smart young woman and easily capable of defending herself. I would be happy to arrange a meeting, if he could let me know what would be a good time for him during my next class. I let Lisa know what he had said, and she handled herself like the young, earnest college student she already seemed to be. When I went to see him after school that day to follow up on their meeting, he somewhat reluctantly admitted that she was a fine young woman and he had doubted her for no reason. I think he really started to hate me that day.

{ 20 }

# The Principal of the Thing

The principal I had been hired by, and taught under for three years, was an old-school administrator, and a damn good one. He had been a high school coach in a small town for many years and when he was nearing retirement he chose to climb up the ladder. This is because retirement income is based on an average of your last three years in the school system. You see this a lot, particularly with men who have been coaches. It's sort of a good old boy network, those plum jobs in admin that can boost the income during retirement to a point that you actually could retire and not have to start a second career to take a vacation now and then.

He was a Spencer Tracy type, down to the round Irish shape of his face and his gruff take-care-of-business attitude. After the new wore off of me, I spent a lot of time trying to get him to laugh, because you never saw him smile. I succeeded a few times, and I could tell that he respected and liked me. He had an assistant principal, also a former coach, but big, young, tall and handsome—a football quarterback type. You could tell that he had a certain reverence for his boss, was happy to be the second in command and learning from a master. The principal also had a devoted secretary, Connie, young, 30ish, who had worked for him since he had come to the district and basically ran the school, the mundane parts of administering a set of large buildings and departments, so that the principal could focus on needs. Needs of parents, needs of students, needs of teachers.

He took care of anything out of the normal day-to-day hum of activity, like that bomb scare. We didn't have an emergency plan yet, nor did any other school in the country. He made all of the decisions on the spot and one-by-one to handle the people, the police, the parents, and when we returned to the school the next day everything was completely back to normal. The feeling in the buildings was calm. That's what a principal is for, not trying to teach every subject. A principal is the center of a school, and a school takes on the personality of its principal. The purpose of a principal is to set the emotional tenor, how it *feels*, how much fun people have, how safe they feel, how respected, how acknowledged, how much they can bend the rules within reason, how much they will be heard, or the negatives, the fear, the disrespect of students as people and teachers as professionals.

I walked into that principal's office one day and plopped down in the guest chair while he was on the phone with a parent. Connie waved me in without knowing he was still on the phone. I motioned did he want me to leave, but he shook his head and pointed to the chair. The conversation was one-sided. The parent was letting off steam about something, and he was holding the phone to his ear and just uh-huhing everything. When she was spent, he thanked her for the call. That probably ended the situation, whatever it was. Just to be heard was all that the parent wanted, to have the principal's ear about something.

Parents are usually problems at the high school level. At the elementary level they are in the school, helping out in the computer lab, doing playground duty so that the teachers can have a decent lunch break, working in the library. At middle school that starts to taper off because the kids are embarrassed to have their parents around their friends. At high school it's completely gone, so the only time we heard from parents is when they were mad about something. They never call up the principal to say I just love the school, you, that teacher, or whatever. They're angry and usually threatening legal action, the greatest fear of any school board. This principal was great at defusing that anger, really listening, and setting up meetings with teachers if that was necessary—but he never just automatically sold out the teacher. He always gave us the benefit of the doubt while he was on the phone with the parent; he assumed that this crazy lady was crazy and not that the teacher actually did what she was describing until a lot of other evidence and testimony had been looked at. If he came to you to set up such a meeting, it was with an attitude of, "I'm so sorry to bother you, but this parent is demanding a meeting about xyz...could you meet at 3pm on Thursday? And can you tell me what she could be talking about?" Imagine that. He actually assumed we were doing our jobs day in and day out—not "Mrs. So-and-so called and told me that you did xyz to little Johnny so now you're in trouble!"

He was a great principal because he defused parents but acknowledged actual problems and worked through them (no lawsuits during his tenure), he *revered* teachers and said often that he could not do what we did, his job was just to make it so that we could do ours, and he was strict with students, like a grumpy old coach. It was a like/hate situation with them. If they were good students, they probably really liked him. If they were miscreants to begin with, he could make it hard on them and let them know that if he had anything to do with it they would not graduate. Serious.

So imagine the change in the school dynamics when he left and Dr. Rapper came. A complete turnaround. By the time that first principal retired, the school had grown to have a senior class and was quite large. For UIL competition, it was a 4A school, which meant that it had a student population under the mega 5A schools, around 2000 students, but was over twice as large as when he had started as a 3A with only two grade levels four years earlier.

When he retired after four years, no one was surprised but everyone was sorry to see him go. Who could blame him, though? He had done what he had planned to do, setting up his retirement to 80% of an administrator's pay instead of a coach's. And he had opened a major big-city school and got it running, by God, which was no picnic. He did leave most of the night work to the assistant principals (he had three by the time he left). They were the ones who had to attend every game, play, band competition, although he of course went to the championships. But it was a very high stress job and dangerous to boot. He was hit in the face and got a busted lip from a 6-foot tall student off his meds. I'm sure he received threats as well. The job is not what it used to be.

So it was no surprise when the announcement was made at the very end of the school year that he was leaving over the summer. It was up to the district and the school board to replace him quickly so he could spend some time with the replacement. They chose Dr. M, a 30-year old professional speaker. Oh, he was on his way to a professional speaking career; the principal thing was a rung on the ladder. He knew it all.

This new principal was African American, which aligned with a good portion of our student population, and I think that had something to do with his hiring. He was huge, about 6½ feet tall and at least 350 pounds. He was young and energetic, so he bounced across the stage when he used rap to communicate not just with the students, but also in assemblies with parents and even at our first meeting with the teachers. You could have knocked us over with a feather when he broke into rap to address us about education. We all walked out of the auditorium with that wide-eyed I'm-not-going-to-laugh look and hurried to our classrooms, ready to do anything to give him a chance, but shocked at his choice of introductions. We were no strangers to multicultural diversity. Diversity is one thing, inappropriate communication choice is another. And as a speech teacher, I can tell you that understanding your audience is critical.

He had come from another large Texas school district where he had served for a year as an assistant principal, I believe near Dallas or Houston. He had no family in our area, and drove a huge black Chevy Expedition, the largest passenger vehicle sold at the time. The black students loved him, for the most part. He charmed them with the rap at the first assembly and slapped hands and high-fived them in the halls. But not the white kids, not the Asian kids, not the middle-Eastern kids. And not the teachers. Even though he had a book of Jonathan Kozol's open on his desk on a Lucite book stand where the guest chair had a view of the spine and title (the page never changed).

He didn't like me. He didn't like the fact that I wanted to buy Macs, even though I had them in my budget authorized from the year before, he didn't like the way I treated my students as though they were young adults, even called them children when he spoke to me about them. He sent terse emails in all caps that would so puzzle me as to why he was so pissed off that I would show them to my friend the theatre teacher to get her read on them before I responded. I finally quit responding to his emails by email, and would just go to his office to talk to him instead.

He was a micromanager, believing that he knew better than any teacher of any subject how to teach his/her class. That he was there to teach and instruct us, I suppose because he had a doctorate. But let me ask you something. If you have a doctorate, which takes four years beyond a bachelor's degree—two for the masters and two for the phD—and you have worked in a school system for at least two years after that as an administrator, just how long have you been in the classroom at the age of 30? Three years would be a generous estimate.

I thought I was an excellent teacher at three years. I thought I was at two and browbeat the assistant principal to give me excellent scores on my evaluation. But I would never, *never*, have presumed that I knew enough to tell a teacher with 5, 10, 20 years of classroom management under their belt what they should be teaching and how. Dr. M did, though, and you could hear in the lounges and halls how the teachers yearned for the old principal's return or someone like him, someone who respected teachers as professionals at what they do and felt that a principal's job was to provide the environment for them to work with the students. To be an administrator, not an education professor. To set the emotional tone of the school as a place where kids and teachers are safe, bullshit is not allowed, and learning takes place.

# Part Three
# What's Wrong

# { 21 }

# Admin vs Teacher

ALL teachers, without exception, who are thinking of leaving education or who have already, have agreed with me that the main reason to leave is lack of control over your work. And of course, the control is wielded by Administration.

Once I had the video studio up and running, we used it for all sorts of things. We planned to tape all of the football games, for the coaches' use in practice and so that we could do an end of the year tape for them. Then we thought we should do a senior tape with everyone in the senior class in it, sort of a journal of their last year at high school. This was a big undertaking; there were about 500 seniors, and although some of them were the popular ones and were everywhere to have their picture taken, some were quiet and hardly ever noticed so we had to use a checklist and seek them out to make sure we got everyone. Whenever the kids were at a loss for what to do in the video class, they had finished their part of whatever project they were on and could get a camera, they went out into the school to get more video clips of students.

The first football game took us by surprise, though. I had only given some thought to the football tape idea, and then with school starting and getting everything else going, I got distracted. All of a sudden, here it was, Friday afternoon before the first game. One of the students asked if we were going to tape it, and we didn't have enough batteries and videotape to do it. We also needed headset microphones to talk to each other about who was shooting what. We had just received the cameras that week, so only had what had come with them, a short tape and one battery. I got the students lined up to tape on three cameras, one from each end and one at the 50-yardline.

The girl who was going to tape the first half on the 50-yardline was very cute. During the game I asked her, "Do you know about football and what to shoot?"

"Well, I know that there are two halves and a show in the middle!"

"You'll do fine. Try to stay out of the way if the players start coming for you on the sideline. If you break this camera, I'll have to kill you."

"Okay, Miss!"

I ran out during my planning period, the last period of the day, and bought the tape and batteries we would need. I had to search for the microphone headsets. We felt so cool wearing them. At this point, only Madonna had been seen in public with one on.

We taped that game and the halftime show, which was magnificent. I'll have to say, I've never cared that much for football but the band director of that school was the best in the state, and it's a big state. We had a big stadium since everyone knew the school would grow to 5A. But as 3A, the teams we played were other 3A teams from tiny Texas towns around Austin, little bitty schools with their parents huddled into one section of the visitor bleachers with four other sections left blank. At halftime, the other team's band came out to play a number and march on the field. There were less than twenty of them. They made a valiant effort, and we cheered them as if they were huge. But when our band came out, they filled up the entire football field with intricate marching patterns, up-to-the-minute numbers, a drum corps, baton twirlers, a girls dancing troupe, and props like huge columns. It was majestic, and it was no wonder that Band was a very popular activity at the school.

And the cheerleaders! I think there were about eighteen of them, girls who had been in gymnastics all of their lives and this was their last hurrah. In gymnastics, you have two paths, both short. You either go into competition and head for the Olympics, spending your days at the gymnastics school, or you try out for cheerleader at your school and continue to get a little bit of gymnastics instruction but mostly dance. Plus, you get to strut around in your panel-pleated microskirt and bloomers all day every game day. Either way, it's about over by age eighteen unless you become a cheerleader for a university, and that usually means a career in dance education afterward.

We dubbed the tapes to VHS for the coaches and band directors, and they were thrilled to get them. The next week, I submitted an expense report to get paid back the $200 I had spent of my own money to get the batteries, tapes and headsets. A couple of days later, the assistant principal, formerly a friendly colleague of mine before she was promoted from teaching to administration, sent me an email that unfortunately, they would not be able to reimburse me for those funds. I had not filled out the proper form; there was a new form that year that had been designed by a bookkeeper there at the school. It was called a 'Preapproval for Reimbursement' form.

Normally, when you wanted to spend money from your budget, you filled out a Purchase Order or "P.O." It required four signatures. I knew about the new form from the in-service at the beginning of the year, but it also required the same four signatures: my department chair, the assistant principal who was in charge of my department, the principal and the bookkeeper. All of whom were supposed to make sure that the funds were actually budgeted before signing. On that Friday when I realized I needed to get the videotape and batteries within hours, I admit I made the decision not to spend the time chasing signatures for the form. I thought that I would probably get my hand slapped, be told to do it the right way next time, but get my money and go on. I was stunned by the idea that they thought they could keep a teacher's money, and determined that it was not right.

I went to meet with the assistant principal, to explain the situation that caused me to abandon the use of the form. She said that she would study it and get back with me. Two days later, she sent an email that the determination not to reimburse me would stand. Not okay.

I went to the new principal, to let him know what was going on and get him to intercede. He said that my explanation sounded reasonable, he understood why I had done it, and he would talk to his assistant principal and get back with me. Two days later he, too, said that the previous decision would stand. I let him know in person that I would have to go over his head and go to the district; it was simply not fair to take $200 worth of equipment from a teacher for the school's use and not repay her for it. He said, "Well, you've got to do what you've got to do," clearly annoyed that I wouldn't just agree to his mandate. But by God, you can't just take money out of a teacher's pocket.

I went to the superintendent's office at the administration building across town. I knew the superintendent because I had been voted by the other teachers in the school to be their district representative. I spoke briefly to her about the issue, and she referred me to her assistant superintendent, who handled all personnel issues. I was given an appointment to meet with him in a couple of days. I came back then and was led to his office to wait for him. On all four walls were Star Trek posters. Big ones. Framed. I had nothing in common with a Trekkie and was worried my $200 was lost. Luckily when he came in and introduced himself, he was fine. He reminded me of Bill Clinton, and he was very cordial. I outlined the reason I was there, and he said, "Was the money in your budget?" I said yes, and he said, "Okay, we'll take care of it."

The next thing I heard about it was from the assistant principal, in an email that I could pick up my check in the office. The email was brief, no explanation, no "And next time, use the form," or anything else. As far as I was concerned, that was that.

{ 22 }

# In. Your. File.

Teacher evaluations are completed by the principal and assistant principals, in which they score each teacher on a number of areas including a classroom teaching evaluation for which you must turn in a lesson plan in advance. It takes them quite a while to complete this task, since they are overworked just running the place and now they have to go sit in a couple of classrooms a day and write reports on about 150 teachers. My first year, my evaluator was the big young assistant principal who worked with the old principal. He came into one of my speech classes and the kids were doing speeches and being videotaped so that they could write a self-analysis. One of the speeches he saw was the 'extra' one with the one student standing behind the other providing the gestures for the one in front. He laughed along with us, we all had a great time, and I received 'excellent' evaluation scores in all but three areas out of ten, with 'good' in all the rest. I thought that was pretty good for my first year.

The second year, it was down to two less than excellent, but I really wanted to get that 'excellent' across the board. I'm just that type. I was so grade-driven as a student that I would do extra credit to bring an A up to an A-plus. Very self-competitive. That year, my evaluation was completed by one of the two new additional assistant principals. I liked him, he was a bit like the old principal in that he had been a very successful baseball coach in a small town and had come to the big city and an admin job to get his salary up higher before he retired. Sometimes I thought none of these guys knew what they were getting into, with the gangs and the fights of a big school. I told him that I wanted to rank excellent in every category, and he told me that he would be ranked down in his own evaluation if he did that; that they were supposed to exhibit discernment by being able to find room for improvement in every teacher, and although they believed that they had some of the best teachers in the area, his job was to not turn in a bunch of 10-10-10 evaluations. Especially for a teacher who had not been in education very long. I understood that; and it was okay for a couple of years.

But that last year I had four years of experience, I did my own class evaluations with the students every year (students were not usually asked what they thought of the teacher or the class in public school, not until college), and received excellent scores from them. I had no parent complaints, and in fact had a number of nice notes from parents about what it meant to them that I had believed in their son or daughter or taught them something that impacted them as humans. My peers had elected me to represent them at the district level. I really wanted that full-blown excellent score.

When he sat down with me to go over the evaluation, I had excellent scores in all but one area. Communication with Administration. I asked him why, and pointed out that I had been elected by my peers to represent them at the district level. He said, "Well, there is something in your file about going over someone's head on a budget issue. That you didn't follow the chain of command."

In. My. File.

The mysterious file that no teacher ever sees or can respond to. First, I told him my side of the issue, about having to use $200 of my own money to buy the tapes and headsets for the first game that year at the last minute, not filling out the 'Preapproval' form and getting the four signatures, then requesting reimbursement and being denied, and finally telling the principal I was not satisfied with the response and I would have to go higher, to the district. I absolutely followed the chain of command, it's just that some of the links didn't like the outcome.

But then, I asked if there was anything else In. My. File. Was there anything about how my husband installed a wall of mirrors in the dance studio that he took out of a remodeling job he was doing? How he built the first set we had in the video department and I paid for the materials? How I had one of our friends, one of the largest painting contractors in the state, send a crew to remove graffiti that had been painted on our beautiful new limestone sign at the front of the school and treat it so that it couldn't be defaced like that again—at no charge? How many extra hours I had worked cooking for the speech tournament and making it a popular choice on the circuit for teachers from around the state? Or taping the football games, creating the senior tape? Anything about how I had worked over a summer installing ceiling insulation and wall coverings to make the studio functional, or personally persuaded the district to pay for those materials above and beyond the school's budget?

Of course not. The File is only for negative comments, positive ones do not have a place to be recorded.

"Well," I said, "I'm going to write up these things so that you can put them in my file. If I do that, will you put them in?"

"Sure," he said, "but it won't change this evaluation."

I'm going to start keeping a file on you guys, I thought.

## { 23 }

# Relevance

"I love your class, it's all I want to do at school. I can't stand going to the math class after this, I'll never use algebra."

My reply:

Back in my day as a public school student, the 1960s and 70s, educators felt there was a specific curriculum you could be taught to be considered educated. A canon, if you will, of math, science, English, and social studies. English, for example, had its American Lit, British Lit, essay-writing, and basic researching skills like use of the card catalogue, the Dewey decimal system, periodicals and books, footnoting their use within your writing, etc.

(I have always LOVED the Dewey decimal system. It's comforting to think that you can put all of knowledge into groups and number them for easy reference. And the card catalogue! What an incredible piece of craftsmanship, the smooth maple cabinet with the perfect little drawers that glide in and out with the satisfying yet small muffled thok! when they slide flush into the cabinet.)

So why is all of this *relevant*? When those kids told me they saw no need in learning algebra, I would tell them about when I was growing up there was a set basket of knowledge that schools would provide and if you went to all of those classes, school was successful. You were educated. In the past thirty years or so, the amount of information has ramped up so much and the rate at which it multiplies has grown exponentially, so that now there is no way anyone could settle on a group of facts to provide that would hold you in good stead in the future. So what we do is teach you *how* to learn. We cannot know what you will need to learn, but we can teach you how to think, how to solve problems, how to research to find answers, and how to communicate what you need and what you know with others. Algebra is a way to think, a way to solve problems by recognizing equations. In the future, you will be presented with problems. They may not even have numbers in them. They may have words, in which case we call it logic. So if A equals B, and if I add C to A, I have to add C or something very like it to B to achieve the same result.

When I explained it this way, the students grabbed it immediately, and were then satisfied to go off to algebra class as a useful activity. If only math teachers were able to explain the relevance of their subject the same way. Because that's what you have to do with education: make it relevant and make it explicit *that it is relevant*, all the time. Just think about yourself. What would it take for you to want to sit your butt in a chair and listen to someone else?

It would have to be to get something you could use in your life, something relevant.

Once I applied for a job teaching adult education. I now am quite happy doing that in the real estate industry, but this was in an area I had no real expertise in, medical. It was a communications class, though, so it wasn't too great a stretch. The interviewers asked me, "What makes you think you can teach adults if you have only taught high school?" And I quickly answered that it doesn't matter what you are teaching, or whom, whether it is a class of kindergartners or adults, age 5 or 55. You have to make it relevant, and you have to make that relevance explicit. You have to tell them, "This is relevant to you because...you will use this in this type of situation..." Otherwise you'll lose them. If they can't see how they can use it, they glaze over and you become like Charlie Brown's teacher: "Mwaaaah, mwah mwah mwah mwah," like a muffled trombone.

We need to teach math teachers, and all teachers, that making it real, making it relevant, is what matters to students, and if they can't do that with their subject material, maybe they shouldn't be teaching it. Look for another way to get it across, something that makes sense to the person in the seat, not just learning abstract knowledge for its own sake.

Once I thought up a speech in which the speaker identified with an object and told us why, like "discovering your metaphor." I wanted to make them think symbolically. They didn't all get it, and limiting the metaphor to an object you could carry in to school didn't really open up the world of imagery to them as I had hoped. It worked, but didn't end up the class favorite some of the others did.

To get the idea across, I did the assignment myself. My metaphor was a set of battery cables because I am a connector. I connect people to ideas, to resources, to other people, to themselves. And there is a spark, an energy involved. I bought a new, clean battery cable for my visual aid and after the speech it became a decoration for my classroom, displayed along the top of the whiteboard to generate the question of why it was there. It gave me a chance to let them know how I thought about my job—not as a parent-child relationship, or master-servant, nor anything else that put me higher than them, but on the same level. A tool for them to use to learn, to understand, to connect.

# { 24 }

# Screeching Halt

We got into a time crunch at the end of the fourth year when we were trying to edit those five hundred students into a 90-minute program. We planned to sell the senior tape and use the profits for the video program. Each student's video clip required two cuts, one at the beginning and one at the end, then placing it into the master tape resulting in 1000 cuts to make, plus music, credits, and the graphics of putting each student's name at the corner of his/her clip. It was a huge project. The kids worked on it as much as they could during class, but it could only be on the big computer with enough storage capacity so only one could work at a time. I ended up working on the final edit for three days after the students were done with school to get it done and to the duplicator in time. Editing video is extremely absorbing. I was there on a Saturday and had been working for a while when I thought to myself, "Gee, I really ought to go get lunch, I'm getting hungry and its probably about lunchtime." It was 6pm.

The students took orders at lunch and between classes for a week prior to the end of school, and I planned to mail the VHS tapes. I took the master digital tape and all of the blank VHS tapes to the duplicator by the end of school. I had purchased all of the postage, the padded envelopes, and printed the labels to mail them. I was hoping the duplicator would have them done before my family and I left on a vacation to Asheville, NC. We were thinking of moving there, and I wanted to be there for a teacher job fair. But the duplicator said it would take longer, so I had to drop off the mailing materials to Lisa, the very capable student who had the misunderstanding with the principal earlier in the year.

On vacation, I kept calling her to check on the status of the shipping. She kept me up to date. It was a big undertaking, 250 tapes to label, place in a padded envelope, label the envelope for mailing, and take them all to the post office. She agreed to get them done in three days, all while I was gone, and was successful in doing it.

The day I returned, I got a call from a former student who asked if I had looked at the tape. I replied that of course I had. I had put it together. She said no, I needed to see the end. There was extra footage after the end of the senior tape. The bottom sank out of my stomach. I viewed the tape and sure enough, there was footage of that girl and others in one of the editing rooms with the door closed, with her sitting on a countertop and basically going on and on about how she had smoked pot and hated her parents. Bad, but not actually graphic depictions of these activities.

The shoot was part of their final project in video, for which these students had not prepared. They were just shooting some footage hoping that they could put something together out of it. They ultimately abandoned it, put together something else that was no good either, and barely passed. Video wasn't a silver bullet. Even hand-picked teenagers can go off the rails, floating along, barely completing the assignments to pass, and not planning nor taking advantage of the incredible gift of the studio and equipment.

Since this was a very-low-budget video studio, we used tapes over and over and over, dubbing off onto the computer the part we wanted to work with. This footage just happened to be on the end of the 90-minute tape that I used to dub the completed 85-minute senior video back onto. After the credits, after the music faded out, there was a black frame and then this unauthorized footage came up. And I had sent out 250 copies, mostly to parents.

I immediately called the principal and told him that I had made a horrible mistake; I described the situation to him. He said, "Well, that's bad but not terrible, it was an obvious mistake. You were trying to do the right thing." I offered to make correct copies of the video at my own expense and send them out with apology letters as quickly as possible. He thought that was a good idea. He appreciated my willingness to control the damage and to do so at my own expense. He told me to do what I could but not to worry; the district would stand behind me.

I contacted the duplicating company and told the owner what had happened. I asked him if he had noticed the footage at the end of the tapes he had made before. He said yes and he thought it was a strange ending, not one a highly professional teacher like me would allow. I asked him why he didn't say anything about it, and he said he was just very sorry. He recorded the new tapes for me in one day at his cost.

I called the student who had called me to alert me about the end of the tape. I asked her how she found out about it and she said that she had received several calls, and her mom had as well. She was very upset with me, and said she could really get in trouble. I let her know in no uncertain terms that she was paying the price for her indiscretion and the stupidity of taping testimony about it, and that far beyond "trouble," this kind of thing could be a career-ender for me. My only fault was the stupidity of sending the damn things out without reviewing them. And the thing about this student was she loved me, had taken several classes with me, stayed late to work on some projects and enjoyed the shoots. I thought she was a sharp young woman but was slipping into the pot-smoking crowd. I hoped that she would straighten up in college, where I knew she would go and thrive. She was very smart, and very bored.

I wrote a letter to go out immediately to all of the people who had purchased the video. I apologized in the letter for any confusion, explained that the tape had some footage on it that was an error, and offered to come and pick up the first tape when delivering the second. I let them know that the correct version would be in the mail within two days. I had the principal approve the letter and sent them out. No one called to let me come and pick up their tape.

Two days later I picked up the videos, packaged and mailed them. I had done everything I could do. The principal called and wanted to see me in his office. "The district has received phone calls from parents who were upset about the tape. Not many, but one vocal one at the school board meeting is all you need to attract the media." That was certainly true, there are reporters who cover the school board meetings for that very reason; to get the scoop on any rumor. "Reba, you could end up with reporters on your lawn, is that what you want? Your family, your children could be affected watching this happen to you. You might never be able to teach again."

Far from standing behind me, the district was making it clear that they would do anything to avoid media attention. I asked him, "What happened to standing behind me? I'm one of your teachers! Wouldn't you say that yes, I did send out the tape with the wrong footage, but it was not enough to lose my job?"

"Well, the tape proves that you were not in control of your students at all times." As though that was possible. Even if you had a classroom that did not include editing rooms with doors, you could not control what students say to each other. It certainly was not the first time a teenager had said their parents didn't understand them. My problem was that it was on tape.

"I'll talk to the superintendent, but the outlook's not good." That darn district, they would do anything to avoid attention. He knew I was a good teacher and he supported me, but the district was more powerful than he was. I got the impression that his support was superficial, and he was for some reason enjoying this. I got it. I went to my car and it hit me. I'm going to lose my job over this! I was very frightened by his image of the reporters on my lawn.

The next day, I went to see him about his discussion with the superintendent. He said they would fire me if I did not resign. His hands were tied. If I resigned now, if anything came up in the school board meeting, the response could be, "That teacher resigned and is no longer with the district." No story here, move along now. If I resigned *now*, he could give me a letter of recommendation. If I resigned *now*, it wouldn't affect my license.

I wrote a letter of resignation with no details, just an effective date, and took it to the principal.

The issue never came up at a school board meeting.

After a couple of weeks of shock wore off, I started looking for another teaching position. I sent my resume out to all of the schools that were in the two districts in my area. Even though I said I would burn off my hair before I taught middle school again, I heard that the middle school in our neighborhood where my son went to school was hiring a theatre teacher. I thought that could be fun, although I knew it would require extra hours to do a play every semester, but not as many as a full-blown musical in high school, since it would just be a one-act play for UIL competition. Still, it would be interesting and I knew what theatre had done for me as a young person. I also liked that it was so nearby; I could walk or ride a bike to work. I interviewed, got the job, and signed the contract.

The next week, the middle school principal called to say that she could not offer me the job, even though we had a contract. I asked her why and she said that someone had said something. "A little birdie." I asked who or what, and she would not tell me anything else. I said it was not fair to make a decision without allowing me to respond to an allegation, but she would not budge. I didn't want to make a problem at my son's school, so I let it drop. I have always wondered who said what about me and if it was the principal himself who sabotaged any shot I had of staying in the teaching field. I started a real estate business and now teach real estate to adults. I continued to apply at schools now and then but got no response.

So that was that. I was done. Two years of college specifically to finish the education degree, four years of teaching, excellent evaluations, respected by my peers, loved by students as someone who really respected them as humans. All for nothing. Well, not for nothing. I am a better speaker now than before the teaching. But I could have joined a Toastmasters Club for that.

## { 25 }

# The Business of School

Part of what is wrong with grade school education is that it is driven by college. Universities are big corporations, make no mistake. They make their money from incoming classes of freshmen and research grants. The huge incoming classes of freshmen are often placed into classes of several hundred people in an auditorium, with no real link to the professor down there on the stage.

The sophomore year is designed to wean out the ones who aren't serious. It's the gatekeeper year. The professors in the research departments don't want the deadwood of students who are not going to be able to provide free help as research assistants when they are juniors and seniors. If you are sweating how much harder it seems to be getting between college years one and two, and thinking that if it gets that much harder in years three and four you'll never make it, hang in there, it will probably be slightly easier in the junior and senior years.

I had a professor of Educational Psychology who was an excellent teacher. She had even written the textbook we were using. Hardbound and published, not some comb-bound local effort. She was only an associate professor though, and could not get tenure. Tenure means you have job security, you don't have to wonder if your contract will be renewed any more. Barring any incidents of illicit activity, you will teach until you retire. You can even have affairs with students, and that doesn't ruin your career at the college level, in fact it's something of a virility badge for males. So this EdPsych teacher had to come up for review every year, for ten years at the time I took her class. The tenure review board turned her down every year, and said within one of the meetings that the reason was "She's just a teacher", meaning she wasn't interested in research, which would bring the university way more money in grants than tuition.

But since tuition in large freshman classes does bring in a lot of money, there is a huge push to make everyone feel like they must go to college. And our society has bought into it to the extent that we hardly have trades taught unless someone has figured out that there could be money made there too, and started a school, like an auto or motorcycle mechanic school, a cosmetology or culinary school. And they have figured out how to get a huge share of that tuition pie.

The thing we use to justify pushing all kids into college after high school is money. A college graduate earns a million dollars more over their lifetime than someone without a degree. (They clearly are not including teachers in that average.) Young people are made to feel inadequate if they are not on the college path. High schools are assessed on the percentage of their graduates going on to college the next year. But is that degree all it's cracked up to be? When I was teaching, my mechanic made twice the money I did, had a beautiful family, went to church and played golf every weekend, and could afford a family vacation once a year. He was successful. He was happy.

Public school has had to eliminate shop class, auto mechanics, and never had the chance to provide plumbing, electrical or most any other trade education. Kids with inclinations in those areas are pushed to enter engineering, which requires college to be valuable of course. To be fair, some schools in west Texas offer horticulture, which could lead to a landscaping business, and culinary education has grown out of the old Home Ec, so people can work in or own restaurants, probably the largest industry in the country.

But people don't have to go to college to be successful. And some people don't do that well sitting in a chair and listening, reading volumes and writing pages and pages. They need to *do*. That's where they're happy, but we've learned to look down on it. This is the effect of the university business, and its voracious appetite for tuition to support the campuses, the stadiums and sports departments that elicit the highest donations from alumni. We should be able to honor those people as highly as those who went to college, if they are doing what they want to do and are good, happy citizens.

# { 26 }

# Special Ed

I think the beginning of the end for trade education in public school was when we decided to stop institutionalizing mentally handicapped people or keeping them home. So much money is spent by school districts on running the Special Ed programs that there is just nothing left for anything else non-academic. Have you ever visited a Special Ed classroom? There are kids in there who will never live on their own, much less have a job. Some will, of course, but the number who are individually attended by an adult aide (at school expense, of course) is shocking. And recently, the Supreme Court ruled that school districts must reimburse parents of developmentally disabled children if they choose to place their child in private school!

I'm not saying that I think we should go back to the dark ages of institutionalizing these children, I'm just saying it's not fair to public education to take up the slack. Schools not only have to provide classrooms, private aides, special bus pick-up and delivery, and teachers at a much lower teacher-student ratio than regular classes, they are also required to count the results of these students on assessment tests for their total assessment results, skewing the true picture of what a school is capable of providing for mainstream students.

It's not surprising that society has foisted off this responsibility onto the schools. Society has also said that schools should teach right vs wrong, sex education, citizenship, and parenting, formerly all taught by the parents themselves. We're just too busy. We're running ourselves ragged working two jobs to provide support for a family that once took only one income. And there is so much TV to watch.

The problem is where to draw the line. If schools eliminated all of the special programs available, I guess my own dyslexic son wouldn't have received the help he needed in fourth grade, when it was discovered that he wasn't progressing in reading as he should have been, and was diagnosed with dyslexia. To fix it, they retaught him how to read, phonetically, but with individual attention instead of in a larger class. It took a couple of years, but he caught up and was able to complete lengthy reading assignments in high school and be considered a decent writer, although he doesn't like either activity.

Part of his dyslexia program was a meeting for parents of dyslexic children. In it, we completed several exercises meant to make us feel what it would be like to be dyslexic. In one we were students in a classroom in which the teacher grew impatient with us for not understanding the questions she was asking while loud, distracting sounds were going on. In another we had to read aloud from a text that was jumbled so that words jumped across each other in a sentence and we had to make it make sense. Several of the parents were visibly shaken after the evening, saying they had no idea what their child was going through. It was an excellent program and should be available everywhere.

It is heartbreaking to see through their eyes, especially if you enjoy reading as a pastime (which they will never have). When I took my son to have his eyes checked for glasses, an astute optician noted that he was flipping the Es and 3s on the eye chart and asked me if I would like to have him tested for dyslexia. In that test, the child reads a text on a computer screen, and a camera on the computer marks and records where his eyes are focusing on the text. Then it's the parent's turn to replay it and see literally through their eyes.

What I saw broke my heart. The red dot that showed my son's focus would start about an inch into a line from the left, and leave off about an inch before the end on the right. This is a common dyslexia issue because they are trying to hurry. They know they are reading slower than others, so this hurrying factor is a coping mechanism. Then, within the lines of text, the red dot read a word, then the next word, then the next, then have to loop back to the first word, go at it again, loop back again, sometimes even have to jump back up a couple of lines because things weren't making sense. It was such a laborious process I was worn out by a paragraph. I sat there and cried.

Understanding what you are reading often depends most on the little words--the ands, buts, ifs, ors, thens, ins, ons. Those are the hardest words for a dyslexic person. Larger words have more clues, and they can reason them out from the context of the rest of the text. The small words are easy to read quickly but get the wrong one in your head, and they often are the key to the sentence. So you have to keep going back to recheck and try to make sense of it.

My child's school had a Special Ed teacher specifically assigned to work with dyslexic kids in two to three person groups. The kids were pulled out of their regular classes on a weekly basis to work with her in another room. In elementary school, the kids just think it's part of school. They don't stigmatize it like they do when they get older in middle or high school. If the problem is not discovered in elementary school, the student will probably not cooperate with being labeled Special by his/her all-important peers. It's just too late.

So I am very grateful for Special Ed when it comes to my kid, as I'm sure every parent with a child with special needs is. I'm just sorry that the expense of maintaining the program that has come to be the catchall for ALL children with needs has forced the elimination of so much for the rest of the students. I wish there was another way, a way to draw a line and say, okay, the kids who will with some help be able to join the mainstream are the responsibility of the school system, but if they don't have a shot at it, they need help from another area of social services.

# { 27 }

# Combat Pay

I once had a chance to talk at great length with a man who had risen through the ranks of a union to become the union president and then negotiator. He also served three governors of his state on their Education Panel, a position that studied many aspects of education in that state. Not the least was teacher satisfaction. During his lengthy tenure on that panel, things really changed. He said when he started, the teachers were concerned about gum under desks. Twenty years later, they are worried about *guns* under desks.

Kids don't just fight each other any more, they kill each other. Back in my day, if there was a fight, kids would get black eyes, maybe a little worse, but they would still be alive. Today, when a fight breaks out, the chance that someone has a knife or even a gun is not small. Unarmed teachers and administrators are often expected to control situations until the cops, or the campus cop if there is one, show up.

One day, there was a girl fight just outside the end of my hall. You always want to know what's happening when you hear people running down the hall. The petite business teacher across the hall from me, who also ran the cheerleader squad, ran out because one of the girls in the fight was her student. That student had her shirt ripped off by the other one. The teacher was about to wade in when I stopped her.

"But all she has on is a bra! What if the other girl pulls that off, too?" she said.

"Let her! Let the naked one remember this for the rest of her life! If you go in there, it could be you without a shirt!" Or worse.

In the spring of 1999, society was rocked by the horror of what kids can do by the murders at Columbine High School. Within days, copycats started creating scare incidents in schools across the country. Ours was one of the first, when a map of the school layout was discovered in a mens' restroom and immediately the principal sent everyone out of the building to the football stadium while a SWAT team was called in to sweep the school and make sure it was safe. We heard the fire drill and assumed that was all it was, so left everything in the school. Once outside, we were told to go to the stadium until further notice. We entered the closest side of the stadium, the home team side, facing the hot April sun.

We got the kids to the bleachers and tried to keep them in their class groups so we could divide responsibility for them in some way. Some fool was trying to hold class in the bleachers, just slightly interrupted by the move from the classroom. She seemed angry at the kids for paying her no attention as she asked them questions about something they had just read in a math class, and continually yelled at them, "Be quiet!"

Good luck! I just sat near mine, waiting, amazed as all the cell phones came out. The students were not supposed to carry cell phones at school, but of course they did and just turned off the ringers. They were all calling their friends and then their parents (in that order) to let them know we had a bomb scare and were now at the football stadium. Great. Now we have parents freaking out and driving to the school to find their baby. Not that I wouldn't have done the same thing, it just increased the chaos when they got there and students started demanding to be allowed to go to their parent's car. The normal checkout process was not possible. How did we know that their parent was in one of the cars? They may have been trying to skip school!!! That would be bad only because we had a sworn duty to babysit their 16- and 17-year-olds and truancy laws to enforce it, so that we and the parents could be in trouble with the law if Jimmy didn't go to school.

The chaos really got started about thirty minutes in, when we realized we needed a plan. Stat. It was hot and getting hotter on those blinkingly bright bleachers in April in Texas. The SWAT team arrived, did a quick search with dogs through the public areas of the building and demanded that all of the male teachers escort them on a locker search. Later, I spoke to a friend who was one of the basketball coaches. He felt that it was a very sexist decision to have chosen the men. They were handed locker keys and they opened every locker, each teacher accompanied by a SWAT team member in full bomb-protective gear with a dog. The teachers were in gym shorts and street clothes, and were wondering just why they had to be the ones in the front of the SWAT guys. To absorb the blast, I guess.

Meanwhile, back at the bleachers, the kids from Special Ed started needing their meds, which were back in the school. When we thought it was just another fire drill the Special Ed teachers didn't pick up all the medications, some for serious behavioral problems. We had some criers and screamers getting tuned up. About that time, parents were starting to show up and were lined up behind the stadium which didn't have a traffic circle designed for quick kid retrieval. They were just stacking up three abreast on a lane and blocking everyone else in, then getting out of their car and coming up to the chain link fence surrounding the stadium area, clinging to it and looking for their child.

Three of us had come down to where the activity was at the end of the bleachers, and decided that we would stand in front of the students to try to have some control over who went out with their parents and were they really going with a parent. This lasted less than five minutes, as we had positioned ourselves poorly at the bottom of two steps down from one sidewalk to the next, which allowed the kids to make a huge crowd only three feet away and looming over us. Looming would have been easy on level ground: these guys were over six feet tall and we were three little five-foot tall teachers. Add to that our two-foot step placement disadvantage and they were three feet taller than us, had a mind of their own, and we had no weapon but our presence and voice to keep them from doing whatever they wanted. We realized it was crazy quickly and gave up.

Ultimately, it became clear that we were going to be there for a very long time, possibly the rest of the day if someone didn't make a decision to send us home. We were just waiting for that official decision so that we could proceed with some normalcy. Since lunch was going to pass soon and everyone was very hot and hungry, word finally came that the school would be closed for the day and we could go home. Of course the teachers at the stadium had to stay until the students were safely off campus. The actual search was completed by about one o'clock and we could re-enter the school for our purses and other things then.

The next day, when we arrived at school everything was in order, everything was back to normal. It was as though nothing had happened the day before. It is testimony to that principal's ability as an administrator that he had that school ready for us to go back to work and was able to publicly calm everyone down—the students, the parents, and the teachers, so that we could go back to work. I heard of other schools in our district that had bomb scares and it knocked them off kilter for two to three days. You may not think that a day is a big deal, but when you have 180 days to teach a subject that normally has about 200 days worth of material, missing a day is tough to make up.

Of course, Columbine wasn't a bomb, it was two boys with guns. It was not the deadliest school shooting, but the deadliest at a high school by students. It caused school districts to enact many new policies, most of which were doomed to ineffectiveness, like zero-tolerance for minor threats (expulsion from school which just makes them angrier and have more reason to attack), metal detectors and cops in schools (shooters don't try to conceal weapons, they waltz in blazing). A study done by the US Secret Service concluded that schools should be paying more attention to the behaviors of students before attacks.

I did have a student who came into my class at second semester one year. Rob was a James Dean type, slouching back in his seat and looking out under heavy-lidded eyes. He seemed older, more mature than the other students, but wasn't older by much and I couldn't put my finger on the real difference. It was not his appearance, but his world-weary behavior. Turns out that he had been expelled a year previous for bringing a gun to school, and his father somehow got him into the Israeli army. ("You want to play with guns? I'll show you playing with guns!") I can imagine that would be difficult for a 17-year old kid and cause them to grow up a whole lot faster.

I was not told about this background. We never received background about our students. It was "confidential" so we didn't really know important facts about whom we had in the classroom. I think this was designed to keep us from treating kids with a certain set of expectations of who they were and having it become a self-fulfilling prophecy. It usually showed up anyway and took us by surprise.

I really liked Rob. He was a test for me. He did not want to interact, and he was in a communications class. I was always trying to find ways that he would complete the assignments. On the first day, when we had an icebreaker activity, the first thing I had them do was say their name, something about themselves that they felt everyone would have in common, and something about themselves that they felt no one else could say. Something like, "I am Mary

Jones, I like dogs, and I don't like pizza." It gets harder as it goes on because they can't repeat anything anyone has said before. The point is that the students find out they have connections with people they didn't know. It is the start to building a real community of those students in that classroom, so that it will be a place they can feel safe standing in front of the room and delivering a speech. I couldn't get Rob to participate. "I don't have anything in common with these people." Finally, after coaxing him for a while, he let us know that he hated school (that was supposed to be the part in common), and, "I have a twelve-pound cock."

My jaw must have hit my chest. I was sure I didn't hear him correctly, until I saw all of the other students open-mouthed and staring as well. "I beg your pardon?"

"I have a twelve-pound cock." At this point, he looked at me slyly and added, "A rooster, Miss." The spell was broken over the class and they roared with laughter. I let that go, what was I to do? He hadn't technically done anything wrong.

Later, we had the How-To speech assigned. Once again, I told them it should be something easy, something they have done hundreds of times if possible since they are not actually teaching us anything, just demonstrating that they can complete the speech. I gave them examples: How to Make Koolaid, How To Make Popcorn in a Microwave.

Rob wouldn't submit a topic. I recommended several very simple ones that had been effective. He watched the first ones, as delivery with thirty kids took three days and he knew he was on the last day. I pestered him about letting me check his notecard outline, though, and gave him until Day Two to have it. I asked him what he liked to do, and he said, "Break things." So I allowed him to do that for his topic. It'll be okay, sort of like the comedian Gallagher, I thought to myself, who makes a living breaking things for entertainment, so I reasoned it wasn't out of the question.

Rob brought in an old computer and a radio, and a sledge-hammer to break them. He followed all the rules for the speech, cleaned up afterwards, and was gratified that the other students really liked it, although his tough image shut down the smile pretty quickly.

During the job interview project, Rob just finally refused to participate. He said, "Miss, I like you and I like this class, but this is just playing games, and I'm not going to do it."

I was livid. This was an activity that took over three weeks to complete. I created it so that it would provide the students with as close to real-world experience as possible, and it would push them to complete it on their own, without the watchful eye of a teacher. I felt that it was meaningful, and this had been borne out by many of the students who had been through it before.

I leaned close to him as the other students were working on their job applications and said, "Rob, you have to do this, it's three assignments plus a major test grade. Give it a chance."

"No, I'll just take the zero."

I was determined that this young man was going to pass my class if I had to drag him through it, and knew that he in particular would benefit from the class possibly more than anyone else in it. I said, "Let's step out in the hallway. NOW."

In the hall, I grabbed him by the shirt at the chest and slammed him against the wall.

"You are going to pass this class, so you have to do this assignment. It's a major test grade, Rob! And I am sick and tired of this game of having to spend so much time with you to get you to do anything in here!" I was really angry and definitely in his face.

He stared at me calmly and then said, "Miss, do you know who I am?"

I loosened my grip on his shirt and replied, "Yes, of course I do."

"No, you don't know anything about me outside of this class?"

"No, why?"

"I was kicked out of this school a year ago for bringing a gun to school. My dad brought me back and begged the principal to let me get a diploma here. The principal said no, didn't want to let me back at all. Finally he said alright, but if there is just ONE thing he hears about me, I'm out, no questions asked." And with that, he turned and walked out of the school toward the parking lot.

I was shaking I was so scared. I went into the classroom where the other students were working and locked the door. I phoned the front desk, "I need an administrator here RIGHT NOW."

"What's wrong, Mrs. Saxon?"

"I may have a student going out to the parking lot to get a gun."

"Okay, we'll get someone down there as soon as possible."

Of course, it took them over ten minutes to come. Rob must have just gone home. After school, I went to the counselors' office to see if I could look at his file. They said no.

I never saw Rob again. That must have been his one thing, or maybe he assumed it was.

The year before that, I had a big goofy kid in my classes. He reminded me of Will Ferrell, so I'll call him Will. The other kids didn't like him very much, although he had his own couple of friends at the school, but I did. He had a good heart. He always meant well, although he sometimes made goofy decisions. Once he put a hot magnet on another kid's neck to make him flinch. It left a red burn mark. It was actually his buddy in the class and they were messing around with each other in the back near my desk while I was at the front of the class lecturing. The magnet was heated up by placing it on my desk lamp, one of those old metal gooseneck lamps. I was very angry with him for hurting that other kid, so without skipping a beat I marched him down to the principal's office and left him there to get a good talking-to. After class I went to the office to see what they had done, and they said that he was gone, taken to the county juvenile detention center.

"No! I didn't mean for that to happen! Can I take it back?"

"Sorry, Reba, but it was classified as assault, and with an assault the law takes over. Our hands are tied. His mom is on the way there, she should be able to get him out." But she couldn't, not until the next day. I felt so terrible that this boy who was just as surprised as anyone that the magnet had even left a red mark had to spend the night with real criminals.

When he came back to school, after a mandatory suspension of three days, he was subdued. I never sent another soul to the office. Later, when I had Rob who was truly dangerous and shouldn't have even been in the school, I thought back to Will, and how the administration could get things so backwards so swiftly.

{ 28 }

# Low Expectations

The sports department usually holds academics sacrosanct. If an athlete fails, the coaches work with them to get them tutored, whatever it takes to get back in grade compliance. No coach would ask a teacher to pass someone whom they had failed, although I'm sure they want to mightily sometimes.

So I was shocked when the principal asked me to do so. I was teaching a class in Multi-Media, for which there was no curriculum. I got it by default, because I had some experience in developing classes for which there was no curriculum. I found a weeks-long tutorial series on Photoshop, so I based much of the class on that framework.

I assigned a research paper on careers in Multi-Media, and since I am an English teacher it was a real research paper: citations, footnotes, etc. I took the class to the computer lab several times to complete their research, guiding them in the process. Two senior football players who had taken the class because it was the only elective they could were clearly just messing around on the internet when we were in the lab. When they turned in their papers, I failed them because they were clearly copied and pasted plagiarism. Since they were on the brink for the whole semester, this failed them for the class.

They didn't think I could prove it, because they didn't think I would or could take the time to find what they had stolen. I didn't have to. There is a way to assess the maturity level of a writing sample based on the number of transitions, clauses, etc. used. I learned this way back in student teaching, when I discovered sentence-combining. It's how you can prove that a student's writing is developing, by scoring earlier and later samples.

The principal came to me and asked me what I could do to "help them pass." Nothing, I told him. They had broken one of the principal rules I had taught regarding plagiarism. That is, avoid it at all costs. And no, just taking someone else's idea and putting it in your own words is not okay. It's still plagiarism. In court when you do it as an adult.

The principal explained very kindly that if they didn't pass a class they wouldn't graduate, and he was ready to have them out of there. Was there anything I could do? Could I let them redo the assignment?

I admired and respected this man, so I allowed them to do it, docking their grade ten points. Since these were not good writers to begin with, I had to give them the lowest possible C to get by. But I had a little less admiration for the principal afterwards.

My older son is very smart, very likeable, wouldn't do homework. When I was growing up, homework wasn't optional. When I came home from school I took a break, had a snack, and by 5pm I was doing my homework. If I just didn't do it, the logical outcome would have been a failing grade in the class. When my son went to middle school and was out from under that single elementary teacher, he shifted into a mode in which he went to class, participated there, took the tests and made Bs on them, but just wouldn't do the homework. He felt like it was just busywork, and in a lot of cases it probably was. But it was repetitive practice that had been deemed necessary to 'get' the new concepts.

He would tell me he had done the homework or didn't have any. Then, when the grades came out, he would have failed something. Every six weeks, usually a different class from the grading period before. And every six weeks, we went in to have the parent-teacher conference, with my son sitting there with us, to discuss the problem. Every conference, he would be sorry, he would do better, he understood that we were all a bunch of adults who wanted to help him.

We grounded him until he brought up the grade, he couldn't watch television, be on the computer, or be with friends. It was generally three weeks, but as short as a week before he could bring home written acknowledgment from the teacher of the now-passing grade. He was a very good athlete, highly coordinated, and enjoyed soccer from the time he was about four. He easily made the team in middle school, played the first six weeks, then lost it with a failing grade, got back to playing, lost it again with a different failed class, just lost momentum and never really was able to play soccer in middle or high schools.

We talked to him until we couldn't think of anything else to say. I cried. My husband would look at me and say, "Why can't you think of anything? You're a teacher!"

And I would tell him, "If I knew how to motivate kids, I would be on the speaker circuit and we would be millionaires." There just is no silver bullet.

My son's teachers all really liked him, which flattered me initially. He was smart, he was funny, he really contributed in discussions. But five years later, in tenth grade at a parent-teacher conference, when a teacher told me how much she really liked him and enjoyed him in her class I told her, "I really wish you didn't. Because he's going to use that to manipulate you into allowing him to do all of the homework he hasn't done on time in the last week of the grading period, and you will give him some credit on it, and he will barely pass the class for the report card."

Once I asked him, "Just tell me what you are doing in the class. Give me a mental picture. When the other kids are going up to the teacher's desk to turn in their homework, are you sleeping, talking to the girl next to you, what?" I wondered if it was embarrassing at all.

And he said, "It's really not that big a deal, Mom, half the kids don't do their homework."

I thought, "Riiiight. He's exaggerating that to make it sound as though it's normal."

So at that tenth grade parent-teacher conference I was talking to two young, particularly earnest teachers of his and I recounted what he had said, to have them refute it in front of him.

When I told them that he said half of the kids didn't do homework, one said, "That's about right." And the other agreed.

I was stunned. I thought that it was like when I was in school, and most students did what they were told, except for the one or two who were going to fail. I asked her, "Why don't you flunk them?"

And she said, "Do you know what would happen to my job if I flunked half my students?"

And everyone I have told that story nodded sadly.

## { 29 }

# Drugs

Drug abuse is such a tired phrase it makes me want to get high to avoid it. Of course there are potheads in middle and high school, and I'm sure in elementary schools as well, although more limited. Hell I smoked grapevines when I was a kid in the country at Granny's, just to see what it would do. If all you had to worry about was some kid falling asleep, that would be good. But of course there's more, and there are the sanctioned prescription drugs required to help abnormally smart people maintain composure in the school culture of lining up and listening.

At the college level, it's estimated that 20% of students are on black-market Adderall. That's not counting the ones who are on it legally. My gripe is not against the drugs *per se*, but against the lack of engagement provided by schools that make the drugs the easy answer.

I know I have mentioned that my younger son is dyslexic, and how school was for him through that lens, but to further complicate matters, he has Attention Deficit

Disorder. Not the one with the H—the Hyperactivity component—thankfully, but definitely ADD.

I remember talking to a real estate client one day about our kids and I said, "You know, I've read that research is showing there is a genetic aspect to who has ADD. But no one in either of our families has it, so we don't know how he got it."

The client looked at me and burst out laughing. "Reba! You're carrying on three different conversations with me at the same time! Of course it's you!"

Well, this caused me to take a new look at the messiness of my desk, just how many projects I have going at once, how few I always seem to be finishing. I'm now sure that if ADD were something in the medical lexicon when I was in school, I would have been diagnosed with it as well. I've just learned coping skills to get along with it (for the most part). I've talked to other adults who know the same thing about themselves. I talked to a school superintendent of a small district about our shared disability, and she said she would come into the office on weekends to write anything important, because she couldn't get deskwork done during the week with all the distractions of the office, the phones ringing, the people in and out.

Diagnosis of ADD is done pharmacologically. That is, there is a part where the doctor reviews the observations of teachers and parents, and interviews and observes the child, but then the doctor prescribes a medication and if it works, that's the confirmation that you have the condition. We tried to avoid this for years. When my son was in kindergarten, his teacher was an old battle-axe who didn't like boys because they were rambunctious. She liked all the girls because they just wanted to play quietly, color, etc. The teacher actually told me this. When I spoke to another parent who had visited the class to help, she told me that she thought the teacher was really pretty hard on my son in particular. We ended up holding him back, having him repeat kindergarten, because the teacher was so insistent that he was just not ready. Not ready to stand in lines for everything, stay in his seat to do deskwork, etc.

He made it through then until fourth grade with some great teachers with a lot of patience. We would ask that he be seated in the front of the room so that when he zoned out she would be able to bring him back. The dyslexia definitely compounded the problem, because when he got lost in reading, his attention wandered off. His fourth grade teacher was the one who pretty much insisted that we have him tested for ADD to see if medication would help. I had been dreading that all of his life, because I just didn't know what the long-term effects would be. Would it affect the way his brain grew? Would it affect his children to take this drug every day? I had tried herbal concoctions, psychological therapy, physical exercises, everything I could to avoid it. Now here it was.

The doctor prescribed Adderall, a time-released form of Ritalin, a stimulant. The odd thing about folks with ADD is that their brain chemistry is opposite; a stimulant seems to calm them down and make them able to concentrate, a depressant would speed them up. The doctor noted that it would take 2-3 days, possibly up to a week, to see the effects. Well, the DAY he started it, the teacher let us know that obviously, that was it. His behavior changed, he was able to concentrate, and completed all tasks quickly.

So we had him on Adderall all through school. Each year when he started school and the pills back up, I gave him the talk about how the drug was only a crutch, that he was supposed to be learning coping skills so that he could get off of it someday. We tried to go without it each year, only to start it up when the grades suffered and the teachers said that yes, he did seem to wander mentally during class. It was so hard to complete homework with him at home after the drug wore off, I knew what they meant. Each time we finally restarted the medication, all problems were solved. He loved school, had no problems completing work in class, and made good grades on that work.

Sometimes I wonder if I made him feel guilty for needing the Adderall by my insistence that he try to get along without it. But that was the goal, to learn how to deal with his own flighty mind. I have with mine, sort of. There was a day when I had put all of our vitamins out in the morning (I administer a lot of vitamins—extra C, E, multi, etc.) and took mine. When I looked down at the little plate I use for this, I realized I had just taken my son's, including the Adderall. I called my husband and told him that I was either going to get a lot done that day or have a heart attack. Turned out I felt terrific and did get a lot done. Diagnosis confirmed.

# Part Four
## What Will Work

# { 30 }

# More Teacher Pay

There are many of us former teachers who ended up in real estate. Teachers make excellent real estate agents because they are smart, tenacious, and genuinely want to help people. I spoke to one about this book and she was a poster child for the five-year mark. Elementary teacher for five years, young single woman, earning $2000 per month in paychecks after deductions for income taxes, teacher retirement system (instead of Social Security), and her 'contribution' toward her health insurance. She worked in the summers at a part-time job, bought a cheap little condo and took in a roommate at $500/month, but still couldn't make ends meet. She did say that she spent about $100/month on her class and students, noticing who really needed clothes or shoes and sending them home with a gift card. Also that she was tired and sick all of the time. Those elementary kids catch everything, don't know how to wash their hands, and just want to love on the teacher. At five years, she gave up. Most current teachers you meet are at the 1-5 year level because almost half of them have quit by five years. A lot of turnover. A few are at seventeen, eighteen years, just waiting to be able to retire and draw that meager pension that they have paid into all those years, that pension fund that has made its managers wealthy on the backs of the teachers.

Once I went to the state building that houses teacher certification and licensure downtown. In the small parking lot, I couldn't find an empty space and the meters were all taken on the street. There was a stretch limousine, running, with the chauffeur in it, parked across three spaces, so I noticed it as I sat in the parking lot for about twenty minutes waiting for someone else to leave and then stalking them for their space. When I finally went inside, I asked the receptionist who was there in the limo. Must be some real celebrity or VIP, I told her. "No, that's just for the guys from TRS, they are on the top floor of the building." TRS is the Teacher Retirement System. They were money managers. I was stunned. They worked for *me*? I asked the receptionist what she thought of them having a limo at their disposal and she said, "Well, you have to look at what they could make somewhere else. They have to treat them like that to get good ones." Too bad they don't look at teachers that way.

Why does society look down on teachers? So many of us are related to a teacher, you would think we would all rise up and say, "Get rid of all those administrators and clerks in the admin building, just get some good ones to run the schools so the teachers can teach and pay the teachers at least the median income everywhere." The teacher in this story went back to school to get her Masters degree, worked on it in the summers, and when she was done she received an additional $500 per *year* for having a masters, or $41/month before taxes. In Texas, where I'm from, the median income for a family of three (say, a single mom with two kids, not unusual for a teacher) is almost $60,000. Starting teachers earned an average of $38,500 in 2007. Teachers who have been teaching for five years made $42,000, so it doesn't get up to par quickly.

They have that all-important degree (with its student loans to pay back), but they don't earn as much as your mechanic, plumber, electrician or any of a number of tradespeople without degrees. But wasn't that the promise? That if you go to college you'll earn more? This is the myth of college, what we tell our kids: If you go to college, you'll earn a million dollars more over your lifetime than someone who doesn't have a degree. We don't add, 'unless you're a teacher.'

People say to me, "Yes, but teachers are only working nine months of the year." Well, let me say this about that. First of all, it's down to two months for the summer break, from mid-June to mid-August, but then yes, when you add Christmas (sorry, "Winter") break, spring break, and all of the other holidays, you do come up to exactly nine months. HOWEVER, I have never seen a teacher who works forty hours per week.

I have a friend who teaches elementary school in a small neighborhood school. She has been there twenty-five years. For the first fifteen years, she was home by 5pm. Gradually, it has ramped up over the past ten years, a half hour at a time, until now when she doesn't get home until 7pm. Eleven-hour days. Every day. This is because she must document specifically what she has taught each child, how that child has responded to it, and compare it to what the standardized tests say that the average/below average/above average ranges would be. And when I say document specifically, you have no idea of the degree of specificity and minutiae that can be dreamed up by the instructional coaches, standardized test creators, and the myriad other positions in the education business that are more highly paid than the teachers.

At the high school level, there is an expectation that you will work extracurricular hours, whether it's coaching a sport or practicing music, band or theatre with productions of full-blown musicals in six weeks of evening rehearsal, set-building, costume construction and coordination with the choir. Or you will have your weekends spent in competitions like debate tournaments or at the very least sponsor a club that meets weekly and has some sort of project that usually takes much more time on the job and away from your family. If you have ever known an English teacher, you know they can be found on most any evening and weekends grading papers. I've even seen them at school basketball games grading in their laps, because they can't get the time to just watch the game but they want to be there and support their students.

Why don't we as a society agree that we want to pay teachers better? I guess it all comes down to self-preservation. It would mean paying more taxes if we were to pay teachers, cops, and firefighters what they were worth to us. Or would it? In the education business, it might be that there is enough money, it's just being spent the wrong way. On too many highly-paid administrators (people are often shocked to learn that superintendents earn 6-figure salaries), too much sports-related equipment and structures, too much of everything that doesn't help the very people who do the actual work.

{ 31 }

# Valuing Education

School should not be mandatory for kids after the age of 16. The US and Italy are the only countries that educate their entire population twelve grades. Those deadbeat boys, the ones who hold back the class with their insistence on being the class clown and pulling the attention away from the class have no business being there. Parents of these kids don't value education, or they are not capable of instilling that value in their children. They are just happy there is something to keep them off the streets and out of real trouble. When you think that in countries where an education is not a given, African children walk miles to the nearest school, Asian families at a poverty level income have even less food and housing so they can pay for private school for their children, and public schools run 9-5 every day, it's shameful what we have come to.

There appears to be no direct correlation between a higher mandatory attendance age and graduation rates. Data from 2004 and 2005 showed that 16 of 28 states that had a "permitted" dropout age of 16 had graduation rates above the national average of 75 percent. "There's just not a lot of good research out there that shows a link," said Kathy Christie, chief of staff of the Education Commission of the States, which provides data to elected officials nationwide.

I believe that if we let them go at sixteen, or for heaven's sake went back to tracking (testing at the eighth grade level that divides students into those who will be on a college path and those who will not, and hopefully have trade schools they could go into at that point), our schools could focus on the academics of people who want them. Managing huge classrooms of people, thirty at a time, that have 10% dead weight just wears the teacher and the other 90% out. 10% of thirty is only three sullen non-cooperative students, and that is probably the norm. But heavens no, we don't want to dash Johnny's chances of an MBA just in case he ever grows up. And we sure don't want to spend the time and effort parenting him to make him understand the value of school.

If you look at dropout rates anywhere in the US, they are higher for people of color—primarily African Americans and Hispanics—than whites. There seems to be a cultural difference in how school is viewed. The majority of teachers are white women (is this why the pay is low?), and this has led to a feeling that school is the domain of "others", not "people like us". That seems to be the excuse for devaluing education. This has not always been true. The American Jewish culture, for example, understood early on that education was the key, and made sure their kids knew it, studied, and behaved themselves in school, even if the teachers weren't from their culture.

This was pointed out to me by a Hispanic woman with whom I worked to get a bond issue passed in Pojoaque, New Mexico. The tiny district had a new elementary school, but the middle and high schools were in poor condition, not remodeled since they were built in the WPA era. The plumbing system in the high school broke down several times a year, and the school would have to close with no restroom facilities available, and not reopen until it was patched. We desperately needed to pass a bond issue to make extensive renovations.

The district was about 50% Native American, 45% Hispanic, and 5% Anglo. The Native Americans lived on the reservation, and did not pay the property taxes that the rest of the community did, so they were unconcerned. That left us to focus on the Hispanic voters.

My Hispanic friend and I started canvassing, and one evening we were bemoaning our results. The adults I had spoken to were opposed to increasing their taxes, period. They themselves had attended the middle and high schools (ten to twenty years earlier), and it was good enough for them, so it was still good enough for their children. I asked my friend, "When I always hear about how Hispanics are all about family, why don't they consider school quality a family issue?" She was just as dejected as I was, so she said, "That's just for show. That's about going to Mass on Sunday and having big family parties. When it comes right down to it, they feel pushed aside by whites" (even though in New Mexico, they had done the same pushing to the Natives when they arrived). "They think that schools are run by whites, and that it may be important, but it is not theirs."

School's answer to this has been to hire brown teachers over whites, to try to shift the balance so that students can identify with their teacher. Affirmative Action for hiring. That's a good idea, and I can see the reasoning for it in elementary school when identification with adults has an impact, but it discounts the noble efforts of white education students who want to commit to the profession and it shouldn't make a difference at the secondary level, when the kid's personality is pretty much formed, and peers are starting to replace adults in importance. Why not just hire the best person for the job, regardless?

One more thing that needs to be said about dropouts and dropout rates: they factor into a school's rating. Students who are not even there any more have an impact on how the public sees the performance of a school. Schools are thus more accountable to society than parents for whether or not students drop out, even though they are past the mandatory age for attendance.

Let them go!

{ 32 }

# School Culture

While at a Leadership Conference for Real Estate in College Station, Texas, I was able to see what a school culture can be. Texas A&M University is in College Station, and the Texas Aggies (from Texas Agricultural and Mechanical College) are brethren (and sistren) in a real sense of the word. I had known Aggies, of course, but they were derided where I lived in Austin, home of UT, the University of Texas Longhorns, A&M's fiercest rivals in all ways—sports of course, but also accomplishments in research, accomplishments of alumni, and automobile decals. Texas is so rooted in pride that Texans also adopt much of their reason for existing from pride in the school they attended, if it was a Texas school. It even expands out to the general population, so that you see folks whom you are pretty sure have never seen the inside of a college classroom decked out in burnt orange Longhorn T-shirts.

But A&M was different, as I had a chance to see firsthand. A couple of years before, there had been a terrible, tragic accident at A&M. In an annual tradition, a bonfire before the UT game meant to fire up spirit, was built up to the height of a three-story building. Something went wrong, and the whole thing came crashing down, killing twelve students who were building it at the time. Texas immediately went into deep mourning. All of Texas, because those kids really mattered, no matter where they went to school. But A&M! And that it happened at Bonfire! Because Bonfire was a tradition, and if Aggies know anything, it's how very important tradition is.

At the conference, I noticed that around town business owners displayed their name and year of graduation on a plaque of some kind in the window of their business. Talking to a retired alumnus, I learned that Aggies often continue to wear their class rings for the rest of their lives, and identify each other by them, striding up to introduce themselves with an outstretched hand, their name, and 'Class of ____' information.

The night I was staying in town for the conference was Muster. This is a tradition of solemn and deeply felt emotion for Aggies around the world. It is a night when Aggies gather in places wherever they can find each other to honor those Aggies who have died in the previous year. In College Station, Texas A&M's main campus, the ceremony is huge. It takes place in the stadium, and candles are lit and placed on the playing field in honor of each of the departed. Their names are called out, and someone in the audience calls out, "Here!" to show that they will always be a part of the culture, the community that is A&M.

Many folks had journeyed to town to take part in Muster at the college. Traffic and lines were long but a feeling of love, honor, and great respect connected all. When I recounted how much I admired the ceremony to my Aggie friend, he told me a story of a few years back, when he was in the airport in Austin waiting for an arrival. A young soldier came in on another plane, and seeing my friend's ring, strode up to him and introduced himself. He then said, "Sir, I just want you to know that we passed Muster in Saddam Hussein's castle."

These are the deep and very human ties of connection that we all yearn for. Texas A&M understood a long time ago that tradition is what inspires us. We have so very few traditions in our society any more. Drivers' license at 16, maybe a quinceneara, then graduation which has become a sort of "School's out!" running of the bulls. But kids yearn for them. The students who took part in the Family Pride project of Melissa's, the ones who dressed up for their part in the Job Fair, all started out cynical disbelievers but in the end, they got prided up and it felt good.

We should look at Texas A&M as a model for establishing cultural traditions around schools, and figure out how to do it at younger levels.

# { 33 }

# Real Teachers

Real teachers teach, they don't 'train'. The teaching profession has suffered from the number of trainers and motivational speakers who call themselves teachers. Teaching is a contact sport, not done well in front of an auditorium where you can't get instant feedback on what the student is getting. It's also, by definition, low-paid: You are not in it for the money.

I have attended 'classes' at various conventions for real estate, real estate investing, etc. Here's how they go: It's a 90-minute class on something you really want to know. You might even wait in line to get in, but you are excited about really learning the tricks of the trade. The first thirty minutes are about what a loser the speaker used to be. They lived in their mother's basement, in a van under the bridge, tried and failed repeatedly. This is meant to make you think, "Gosh, if he can do it, so can I!"

The second thirty minutes is about what a huge success they were once they figured out the information you came to learn. The last thirty minutes is about how very valuable that information is, a $1200 value for four CDs of them talking, maybe with a workbook, yours today only for $400. Or some multiple of those numbers. I have even seen them market their 'killer info' for a thousand bucks or a monthly subscription of several hundred, but it is 'worth' $5000. Here's the secret: You'll never get the information at the seminar. It's just an infomercial in person. Hey, buddy, a good book is still $20. If you really wanted to impact other people's lives and help them, why didn't you just write a book?

Of course, they did write a book, but they are publishing it themselves, and it costs way more than any book in Amazon.com but is available to you today only in the back of the room at a severe discount because they care.

They are charlatans, snake oil salesmen, and it's no coincidence that there are very few women doing it. Women don't tend to be attracted to get-rich-quick schemes or charlatanism as much as men. That's one reason why there are more women teachers than men. That plus the fact that it's convenient when you have small children and you are off work when they are out of school so you don't have to rush around to find temporary day care for Christmas or summer vacations. And you get to spend vacations with your kids. And women are the ones who want this more than men, or at least enough to give up a higher paying career to have it. Finally, I think there's often some mothering involved in good teaching. There is a level of care, not that men don't have, but that they may not be accustomed to using in other businesses.

When I started writing this book, I set up a google alert on the word 'teacher'. That brings into my email box every morning a short description and link to every article that was posted on the internet the previous day, whether online or in newspapers that publish an online edition. Every day, *every day*, there is something about some teacher getting busted for sexually molesting children or teens, physically or in child pornography. Some of them started out as teachers, but somewhere their darker selves took over. Some actually entered the profession to be provided with a ready supply of victims. What level of professionalism do you think you're going to get for the least you can pay?

# Epilogue

I am a real teacher. It's what brings me greater happiness than anything else I could do. When a student says, "I tried what you taught and it *worked!*" it's the best feeling in the world. This book has been your glimpse into the making of a teacher, the very good and the very bad parts of teaching, and what to consider when you think about teaching as a profession. Not just for readers who are considering it for themselves, but also for any member of a society who is thinking about whether to pay them more for what they do, and to keep the best ones in the classroom by respecting them.

## ABOUT THE AUTHOR

Reba Saxon is a natural-born teacher. She has enjoyed the educative experience, whether student or teacher, all of her life. Reba currently teaches adult education on real estate in Texas, and is a real estate broker in the Austin area.

www.ingramcontent.com/pod-product-compliance
Lightning Source LLC
LaVergne TN
LVHW051553070426
835507LV00021B/2560